Follett Social Studies

Our Communities

Program Directors

Phillip Bacon
M. Evelyn Swartz

Authors

Janet E. Alleman-Brooks
James B. Kracht

Allyn and Bacon, Inc., Newton, Massachusetts

*Rockleigh, NJ   Atlanta   Warrensburg, MO   Dallas   Rancho Cordova, CA
London   Sydney   Toronto*

Teacher Consultants

Joan Sánchez Augerot
Seattle Public Schools
Seattle, Washington

Elizabeth G. Charette
West Tampa Middle School
Tampa, Florida

Silvio Guglielmo Benvenuti
Detroit Public Schools
Detroit, Michigan

Carolyn E. Comey
Washington School #6
Phoenix, Arizona

Margaret L. Boyd
Fairfax County Schools
Vienna, Virginia

Patricia DeBardeleben
Treadwell Elementary School
Memphis, Tennessee

Gary L. Caldwell
Omaha Public Schools
Omaha, Nebraska

Jeanette Hadley
Public School 154, Manhattan
New York, New York

ISBN 0-205-09506-2

Printed in the United States of America

1 2 3 4 5 6 7 8 9   93 92 91 90 89 88 87 86 85

Lynne K. Hollomon
Portland Public Schools
Portland, Oregon

Dolores K. Horwitz
William Hibbard School
Chicago, Illinois

Sister St. Rita Marotta, I.H.M.
St. Dorothy School
Drexel Hill, Pennsylvania

Edith Naiser
Spring Branch Schools
Houston, Texas

Helen Rogers
Gary School Corporation
Gary, Indiana

Edith B. Rudder
Wake County Schools
Raleigh, North Carolina

Martha Doerr Toppin
Oak Grove Intermediate School
Concord, California

Ronald J. Walker
William H. Ohrenberger School
Boston, Massachusetts

Table of Contents

Map List

The
Atlas

The World

NORTH

UNITED STATES

AMERICA

Los Angeles

Houston
Gulf of
Mexico

MEXICO

Mexico City ⊛

GUATEMALA

Ottawa ⊛

New York
Philadelphia
Washington, D.C.

Central
America

ATLANTIC

PACIFIC

Equator

OCEAN

SOUTH

Lima ⊛

AMERICA

Rio de Janeiro

Buenos Aires ⊛

LEGEND
—··— International Boundary
⊛   National Capitals
•   Cities

8

ARCTIC   OCEAN

ASIA

Moscow

EUROPE

London

ITALY

Rome

SPAIN

Cairo

CHINA

Peking

JAPAN

Tokyo

INDIA

Calcutta

Hong Kong

PACIFIC

AFRICA

OCEAN

Lagos

Equator

Java

OCEAN

Kinshasa

INDIAN

OCEAN

AUSTRALIA

Cape Town

Canberra

ANTARCTICA

© FPC

9

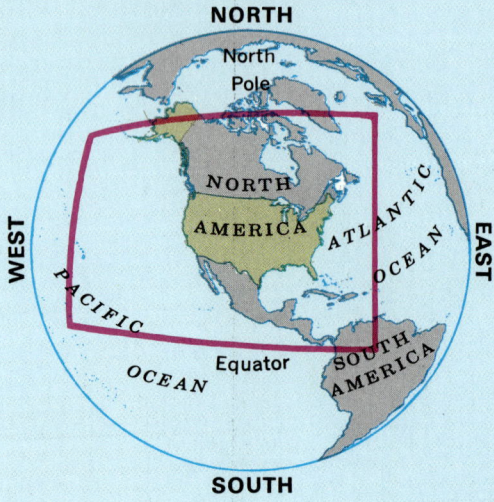

NORTH

North
Pole

NORTH
AMERICA

WEST

EAST

PACIFIC

ATLANTIC

OCEAN

OCEAN

Equator

SOUTH
AMERICA

SOUTH

UNITED
STATES
(ALASKA)

PACIFIC OCEAN

WEST

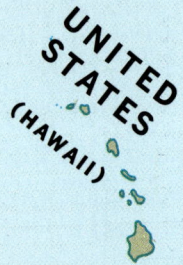

UNITED
STATES
(HAWAII)

NORTH

CANADA

Columbia River
Missouri River
St. Lawrence River
The
Great
Lakes

Great
Salt
Lake

UNITED STATES
OF AMERICA

Ohio River

Colorado
River

Washington, D.C.

EAST

ATLANTIC

OCEAN

Rio Grande

Mississippi River

MEXICO

11

SOUTH

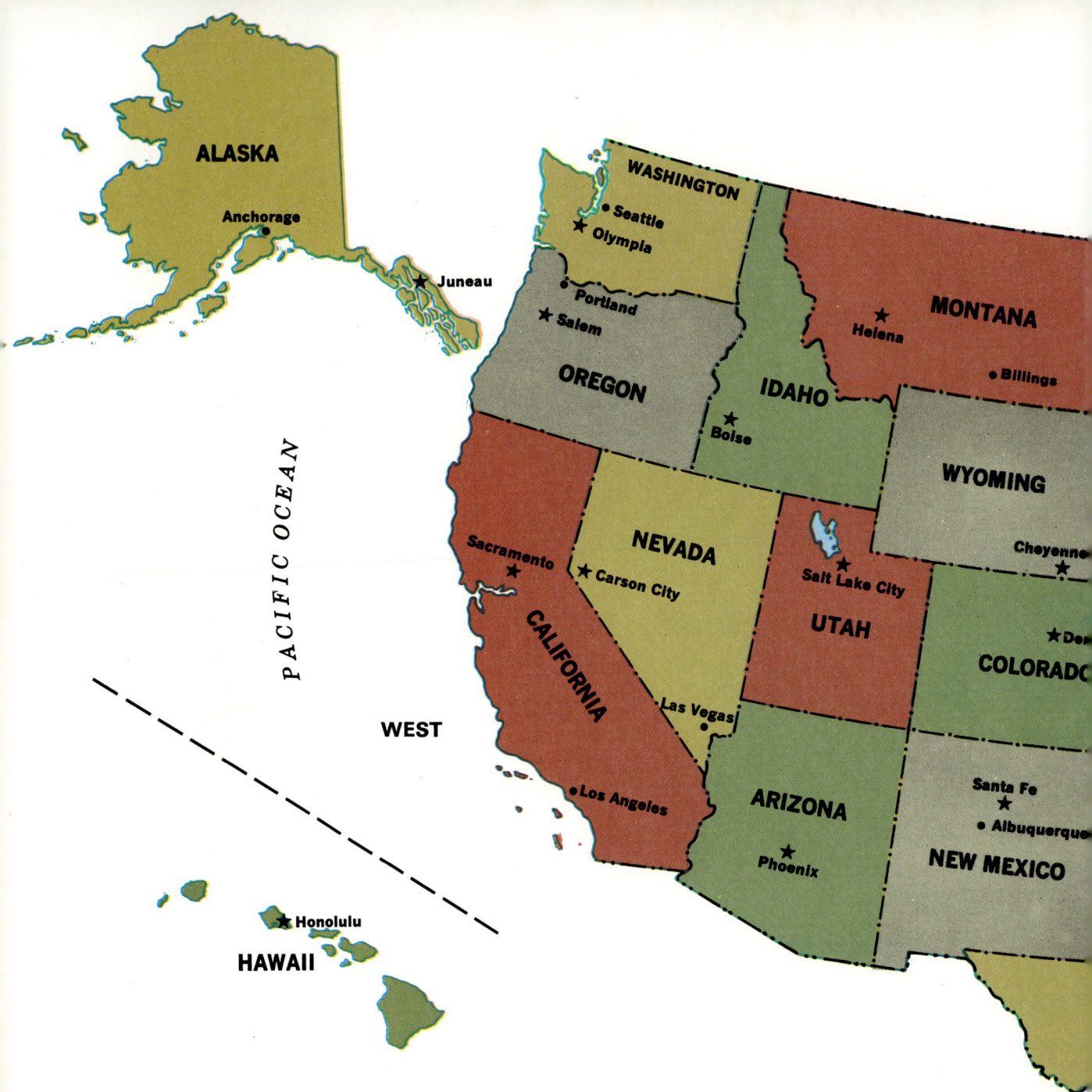

ALASKA

Anchorage

Juneau

WASHINGTON

Seattle

Olympia

Portland

Salem

OREGON

MONTANA

Helena

Billings

IDAHO

Boise

WYOMING

Cheyenne

PACIFIC OCEAN

Sacramento

NEVADA

Carson City

Salt Lake City

UTAH

Des

COLORADO

WEST

CALIFORNIA

Las Vegas

Los Angeles

ARIZONA

Santa Fe

Albuquerque

NEW MEXICO

Phoenix

Honolulu

HAWAII

United States

⊛ Capital of the United States

★ State Capitals

● Largest Cities

—•— State Boundaries

In Some States the Capital
Is the Largest City

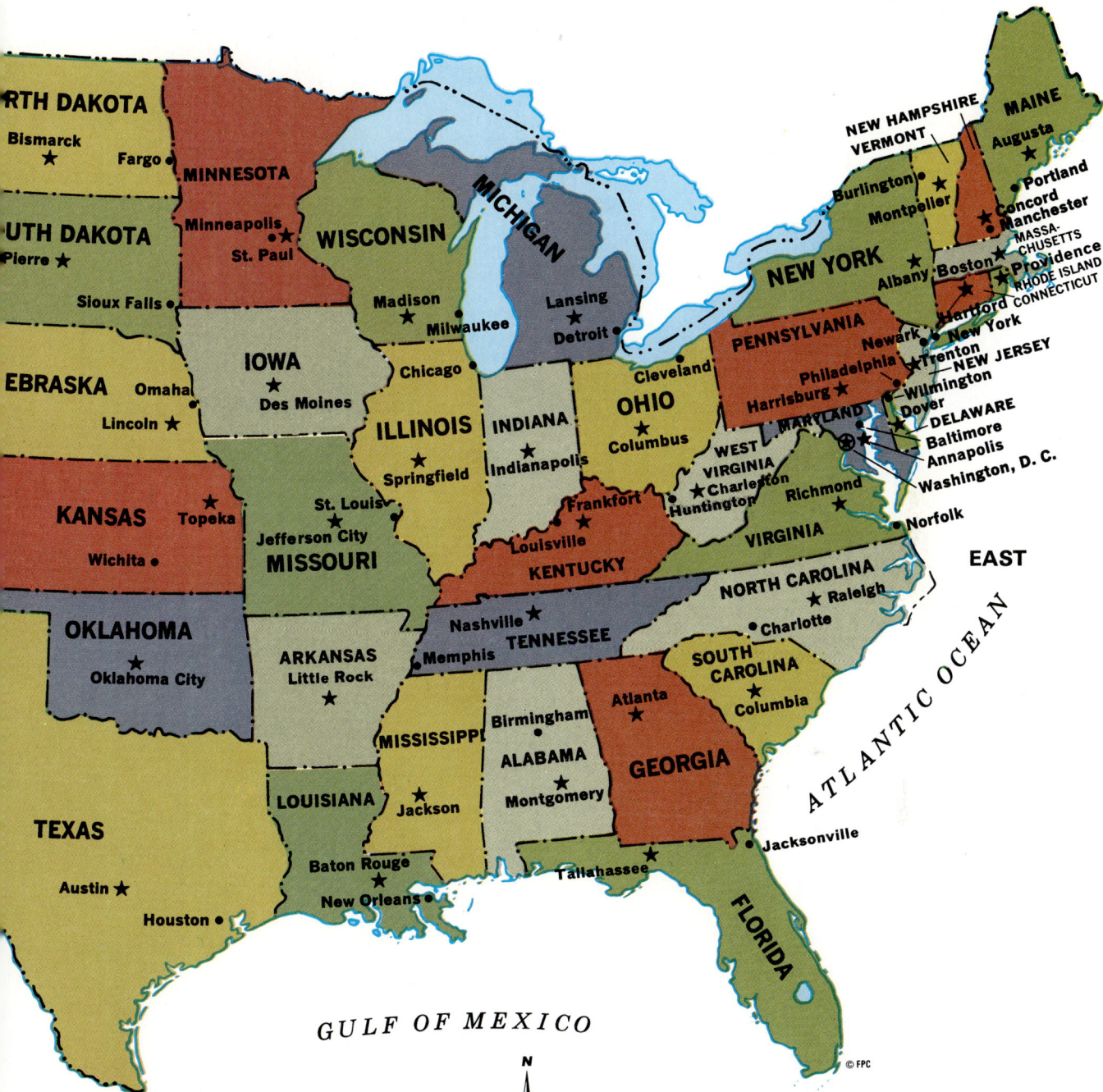

NORTH

RTH DAKOTA
Bismarck ★   Fargo ●

UTH DAKOTA
Pierre ★
Sioux Falls ●

EBRASKA
Omaha ●
Lincoln ★

KANSAS   Topeka ★
Wichita ●

OKLAHOMA
Oklahoma City ★

TEXAS
Austin ★
Houston ●

MINNESOTA
Minneapolis ●★
St. Paul ●

WISCONSIN
Madison ★
Milwaukee ●

IOWA ★
Des Moines

MISSOURI
St. Louis ●
Jefferson City ★

ARKANSAS
Little Rock ★

LOUISIANA
Jackson ★
Baton Rouge ★
New Orleans ★

MICHIGAN
Lansing ★
Detroit ●

ILLINOIS
Springfield ★
Chicago ●

INDIANA
Indianapolis ★

OHIO
Columbus ★
Cleveland ●

KENTUCKY
Frankfort ★
Louisville ●

TENNESSEE
Nashville ★
Memphis ●

MISSISSIPPI
Jackson ★

ALABAMA
Montgomery ★
Birmingham ●

GEORGIA
Atlanta ★
Columbia ★

SOUTH
CAROLINA
Columbia ★

NORTH CAROLINA
Raleigh ★
Charlotte ●

VIRGINIA
Richmond ★
Norfolk ●

WEST
VIRGINIA
Charleston ★
Huntington ●

PENNSYLVANIA
Harrisburg ★

NEW YORK
Albany ★

NEW HAMPSHIRE
VERMONT
Burlington ●
Montpelier ★
Concord ★
Manchester ●

MAINE
Augusta ★
Portland ●

MASSA-
CHUSETTS
Boston ★
Providence ★
RHODE ISLAND
Hartford ★
CONNECTICUT

New York ●
Newark ●
Trenton ★
NEW JERSEY
Philadelphia ●
Wilmington ●
Dover ★
DELAWARE
Baltimore ●
Annapolis ★
MARYLAND
Washington, D. C. ⊕

FLORIDA
Tallahassee ★
Jacksonville ●

ATLANTIC OCEAN

EAST

GULF OF MEXICO

© FPC

SOUTH

N
W   E
S

13

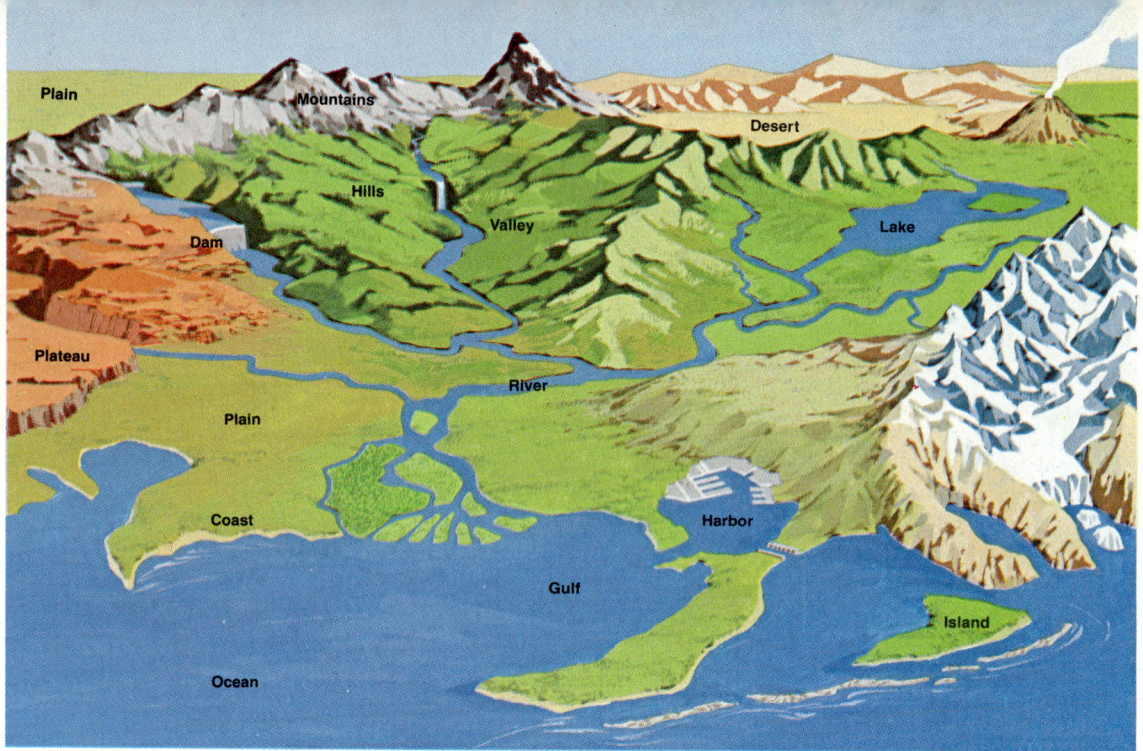

Plain · Mountains · Desert · Hills · Valley · Lake · Dam · Plateau · Plain · River · Coast · Harbor · Gulf · Island · Ocean

A Dictionary of Geographical Words

coast Land along a sea or an ocean.

dam A wall built across a river to stop or slow down the flow of water.

desert A dry area of land where few plants can grow.

gulf Part of a sea or ocean that reaches into the land.

harbor A place where ships may anchor safely.

hill A rounded part of the earth's surface.

island Land that is entirely surrounded by water and smaller than a continent.

lake An inland body of water.

mountain High, rocky land, usually with steep sides and a pointed or rounded top, higher than a hill.

ocean One of earth's four largest bodies of water.

plain An area of broad, level land.

plateau An area of high, flat land.

river A large stream of water flowing through the land.

valley Low land between hills or mountains.

The Atlas Tells a Story

As you read, think about these words.

continent   sphere   equator   symbol

ocean   hemisphere   physical map   key

Look at page 7. The earth is big. Yet it does not look big from thousands of miles out in space. But it does look round. You can see the round shape of the earth in this picture.

Land and Water

A globe is a small model of the earth. Globes show you the land and water on the earth. Look at the globes on this page. The large land areas are called **continents**. The large water areas are called **oceans**.

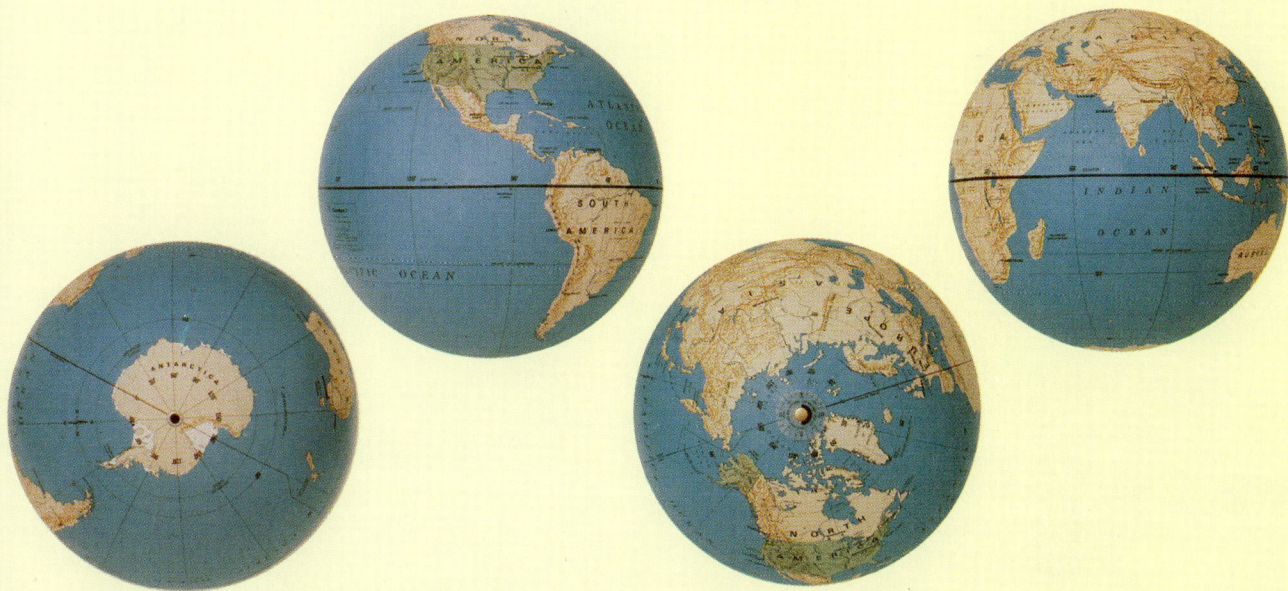

Maps and Globes

Globes are true models of the earth. Globes are true models because they are round like the earth.

Maps are flat. They are not round like the earth. Because maps are flat, they are not the same as globes.

Look at the map of the world on pages 8–9. It shows all the continents and all the oceans. How many continents are there? How many oceans? Name them.

Now look at a globe. What do you have to do to your globe to see all the continents and oceans?

Hemispheres

A globe is sometimes called a **sphere**. The word *sphere* means "a round body." A ball is a sphere. A globe is a sphere. Earth is a sphere.

Each of the pictures on this page shows only half a sphere. The word *hemi* means "half." So each of these pictures shows you a **hemisphere**. The northern half of the earth is called the Northern Hemisphere. The North Pole is the center of the Northern Hemisphere. What is the center of the Southern Hemisphere? A line called the **equator** is found on maps and globes. It is the dividing line for the Northern and Southern Hemispheres.

Look at the map on pages 8–9. Find the equator. In what hemisphere do you find the continent of North America? Europe? Australia?

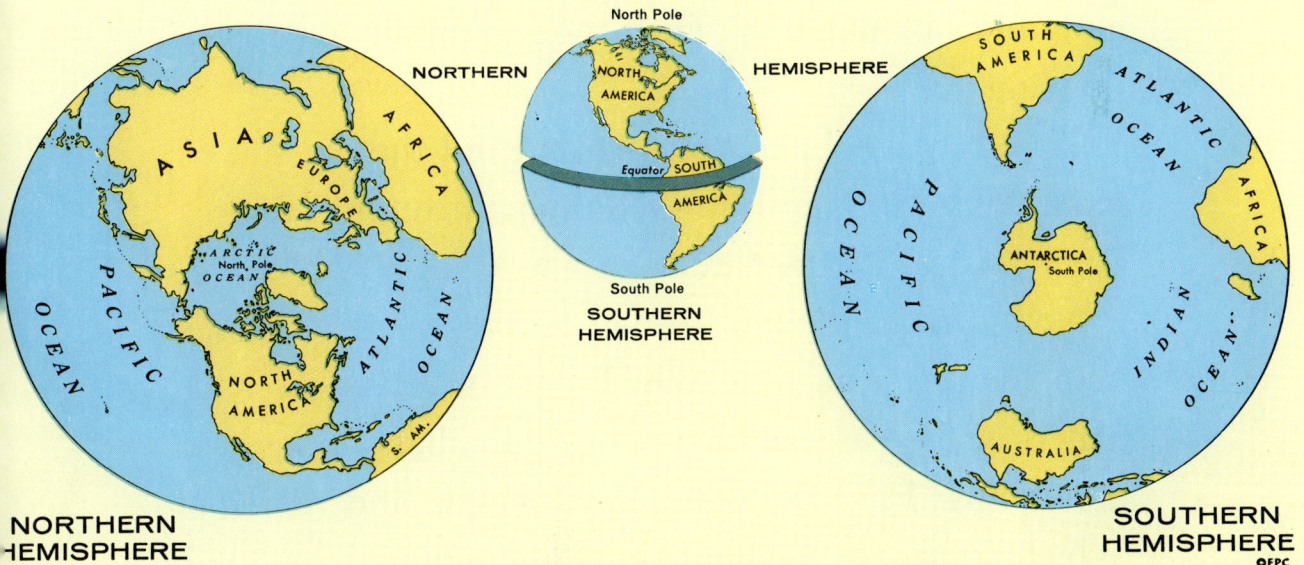

NORTHERN HEMISPHERE

North Pole

NORTH AMERICA

Equator SOUTH AMERICA

South Pole

SOUTHERN HEMISPHERE

NORTHERN HEMISPHERE

SOUTHERN HEMISPHERE

©FPC

17

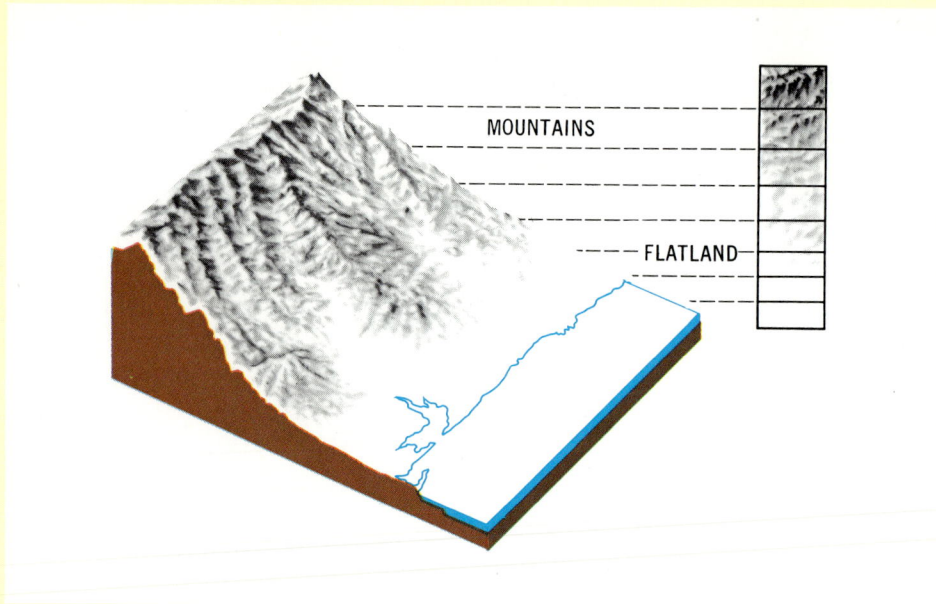

Reading Physical Maps

Look at the drawing on this page. It will help you read some kinds of maps. These maps are called **physical maps**. Such maps help you understand what the land looks like. It tells you whether an area has mountains or flat land. Find the mountains on this drawing.

Turn to page 14 of your Atlas. Find the mountains. How are the mountains different from other land in the picture?

Now turn to the world map on pages 8–9. This map is a physical map. Which part of North America, the eastern or western part, has more mountains? Find the continents of Asia and Africa. Which continent has more mountains?

Map Symbols

Maps use special **symbols** to tell their story. Each symbol stands for something real on the earth. Colors, lines, and dots may be symbols on maps. In order to understand a map, you must know what these symbols mean.

Maps have **keys** to help you unlock the meaning of the symbols. Look at the world map on pages 8–9. The key to this map explains the meaning of these symbols. What are these symbols? What do they mean? Find three places on this map where each is used.

On this page is another key. The symbols look the same as those on pages 8–9. But they mean different things. What does each symbol mean on this key?

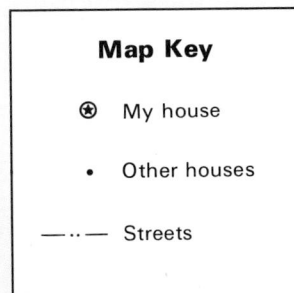

Map Key

⊛   My house

•   Other houses

—··—   Streets

The same symbols can be used to mean different things on different maps. Why do you think it is important always to look at the map key before beginning to read a map? See if you can draw a map using the symbols on this page.

Size and Detail

The two pictures on this page show the same playground. The picture on the left shows a larger part of the playground. Because the picture on the right shows a smaller part of the playground, objects look bigger. We can see more detail.

Large areas, such as the whole world, can be shown on two pages! Look at pages 8–9 again.

Now look at pages 10–11. Here is only part of the world. It is the part in which we live. Two pages have been used to show just one part of the world.

Look now at pages 12–13. Here are the fifty states of our country. These fifty states are smaller than North America. Yet two pages have been used to show only that part of North America that we call the United States of America. Which map shows the largest area? Which map shows the most detail?

Map Keys

Look at the map on pages 12–13. This is a map of our country. What is the name of your state? Find it. What is just west of your state? What is east of your state?

Find the key to this map. What does the symbol ★ stand for? Find the name of the city that this symbol stands for. What does the symbol ★ mean? Find that symbol in your state. What is the name of the city that this symbol stands for in your state?

Look carefully at the line symbol that separates one state from another. Compare it with the line symbol that separates Canada and the United States. How do these symbols differ? Why do you think they are different?

Checking Up

1. Which is a better model of the earth, a map or a globe? Why?
2. Which can show more detail, maps or globes? Why is that?
3. Turn to page 15. Find the new social studies words at the top of the page. Tell what each one means.

Unit 1

People Live
in Many Places

Portland, Oregon, is a city near mountains.

People Everywhere

As You Read

Look for answers to this key question.

How are people around the world the same?

There are many people in the world. They live in many places.

In most ways people are the same.
We need places to live.
We need food and clothes.
We need water and air.
We need people.

Checking Up

1. What answers would you give to the key question at the beginning of this chapter?
2. *Look at the pictures on these pages. How are these places like the place where you live?*

Where Are the People?

As You Read

1. Look for answers to these key questions.
   a. What are three kinds of places where people live?
   b. How are these places different?
2. Use this reading skill.
   When you read, you learn new things. You read words. You can also read pictures. Look at the pictures in this chapter. In what kinds of places do people live?

Where do people live?
Most people live where the land is flat.
Others live near mountains.

Some people live near water.
People live in places all over the world.

Checking Up

1. What answers would you give to the key questions at the beginning of this chapter?

2. *What is the land like where you live? Make a list of words or draw a picture to tell about the land where you live.*

Maps Tell a Story of Landforms

As you read, think about these words.

plain   mountain   hill   plateau   landform

Our world has many kinds of places. Some places are low, flat lands, or **plains**. Some places are **mountains**. Some places are **hills**. Other places are high, flat lands, or **plateaus**. Plains, mountains, hills, and plateaus are **landforms**.

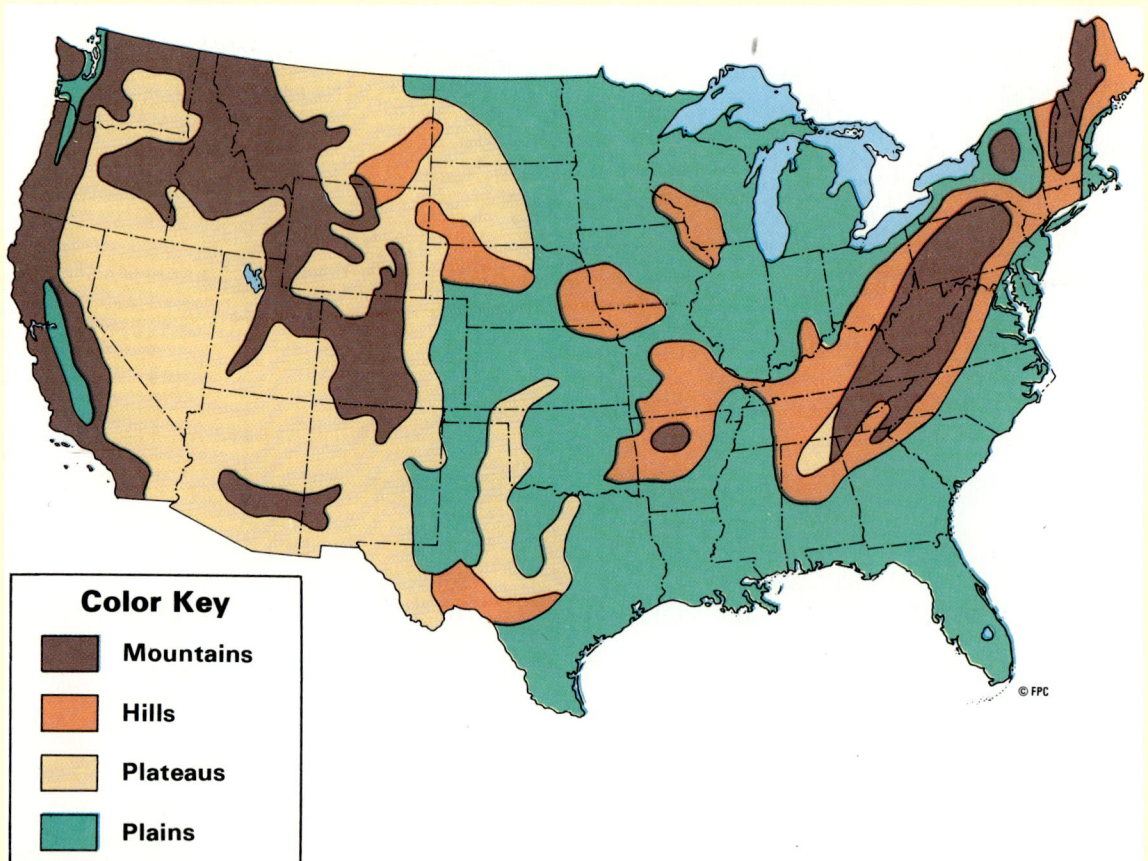

Color Key

- Mountains
- Hills
- Plateaus
- Plains

© FPC

Look at the map of the United States. This map shows where there are mountains, hills, plateaus, and plains. Find the box marked Color Key. The color key tells you how to read the map. Mountains are brown. What color are hills? plateaus? plains?

Find your state on this map. You may use the map on pages 12–13 in the Atlas to help you. What landforms are in your state?

Checking Up

1. Name the four landforms.
2. How are they different from one another?

Different Places, Different Sizes

As You Read

1. Think about these words.
   farm   town   city
2. Look for answers to these key questions.
   a. What are three kinds of places where people live?
   b. Which places have the most people? Which places have the fewest?
3. Use this reading skill.
   This chapter and all following chapters in this book begin with a list of important social studies words. You will also find these words in **bold** type the first time they are used. The Glossary at the back of your book tells you what these words mean. As you finish each chapter, be sure you understand the meaning of each word.

People live in different places.
These places are different sizes.
Some places have many people. Some do not.
Some people live on **farms**.

Some people live in **towns**.

There are more people in a town than on a farm.

There are many different kinds of towns.

Some people live in **cities**.
There are more people in a city than in a town.

There are many different kinds of cities.

A Bus Driver

Have you ever been on a bus? Maybe you ride a bus to school. Maybe you ride a bus in your community. You may have even taken a long trip on a bus.

Some special buses take people on long trips. They take them from town to town and from city to city. They even go from state to state. They pass many kinds of farms. They pass towns and cities.

Checking Up

1. What answers would you give to the key questions at the beginning of this chapter?
2. *How do you think living in a city is different from living on a farm?*

Bus drivers are special people. They must learn many things to do their jobs. They must learn to drive the bus. They must learn all the safety rules. They must read all the safety signs. They must read maps. People need bus drivers. They make trips safe.

Unit 1 Summary

- People everywhere have the same needs.
- People live in many kinds of places.
- People live on farms, in towns, and in cities.
- The places people live are different sizes.

Unit 1 Review Workshop

What Have You Learned?

1. Name three things that people everywhere need.
2. Which has more people, a city or a town?
3. Name the four landforms.

Use Your Reading Skills

Choose a picture from page 31. Make up a story that tells what you read in the picture.

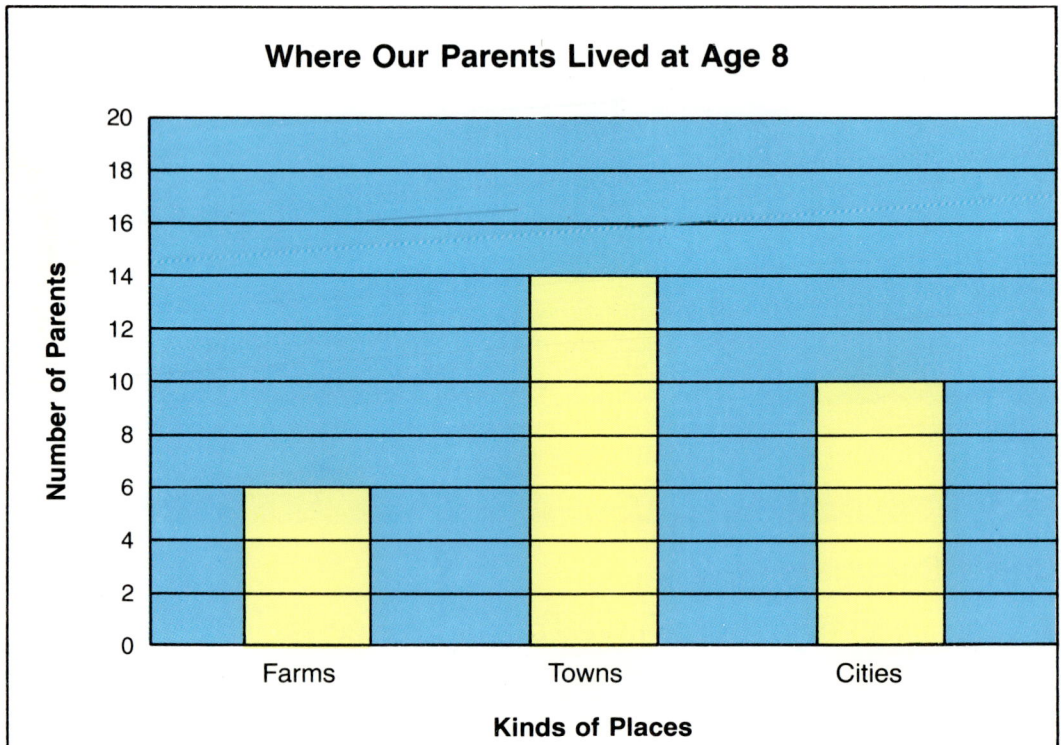

Where Our Parents Lived at Age 8

(Bar graph)

Y-axis: Number of Parents (0, 2, 4, 6, 8, 10, 12, 14, 16, 18, 20)

- Farms: 6
- Towns: 14
- Cities: 10

X-axis: Kinds of Places

Use Your Math Skills

Ask your parents where they lived when they were eight years old: on a farm, in a town, or in a city. Then your teacher will help make a class bar graph. Graphs are a way of showing information. This graph will show you how many parents grew up in each kind of place. You can use the graph to compare where your parents lived when they were your age.

Learn by Doing

Look at old magazines. Cut out four pictures about farms, towns, or cities. Paste them on paper. Under each picture write a sentence that tells if the picture shows a farm, a town, or a city.

This is a picture of a farm.

Unit 2

People Live on Farms

Corn plants grow tall on this farm in Illinois.

The World of Farms

As You Read

1. Think about these words.
   shelter   depend   location
2. Look for answers to these key questions.
   a. How are farms the same?
   b. How are farms different?
3. Use this reading skill.
   Pictures teach us many things. In this book many of the pictures have sentences written under or near them. These sentences are called captions. As you look at the pictures in this book, read the captions to learn more about the pictures.

Many people in our world live on farms.

We need farms. Most of our food comes from farms. Vegetables, fruits, and grains come from farms. Meat, eggs, and milk come from farms. Farmers all over the world work to produce the food that we eat every day.

Some clothes are made of cotton and wool. Cotton is grown on farms. Farmers in some parts of the world raise sheep for wool. What kinds of clothes are made of cotton and wool?

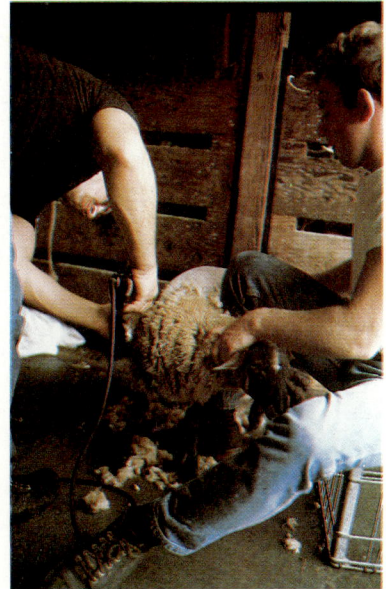

We all need **shelter**, or a place to live. Some
people live in homes made of wood. Much of this
wood comes from tree farms.

Farms all over the world are the same. They help
us meet our needs for food, clothing, and shelter.
Farms are the same in other ways.

Farmers who grow crops prepare the soil and plant seeds. They make sure there is enough water. They hope there will be enough sunshine. Farmers gather their crops when they are ripe.

Farmers who raise animals work to keep the animals healthy. Healthy animals provide food for many people. Many people **depend** on, or need, these animals.

This woman lives in Africa. She and her family use hand tools to farm.

Some farmers use machines to help them with their work.

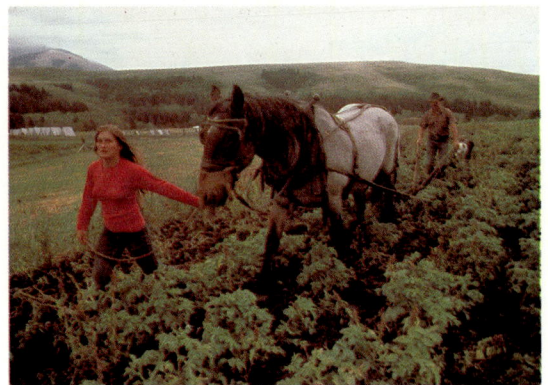

Some farmers use animals to help them with their work.

How do farmers decide what to produce? Often their **location**, or where they live, helps them decide. Farmers choose to grow crops or raise animals that will do well in their location.

People everywhere depend on farmers.

How do these people depend on farms?

Checking Up

1. What are three needs farmers help us meet?
2. What answers would you give to the key questions at the beginning of this chapter?
3. *Why is it important for farmers to care for their crops or animals?*

A Wheat Farm in Kansas

As You Read

1. Think about these words.
   weather   harvest   sell
2. Look for answers to these key questions.
   a. How are machines important to this farm?
   b. How do people use wheat?

The wheat farm in this picture is like many wheat farms in the United States. It is very big. If you stand in the center of this farm, you cannot even see to the end of it.

Wheat is grown on the plains in the middle of the United States. The soil is good for wheat. Wheat can be planted for miles and miles. This farm is in Kansas.

The state of Kansas has many wheat farms like this one. Find Kansas on the map on pages 12–13.

45

The Hoffman family owns this farm. Look again at the picture of their farm on page 45. Where is their house? Where is the barn?

The Hoffmans have machines that help them with their work. One machine prepares the ground for planting. Another machine plants the seeds and covers them.

The Hoffmans know their soil is good. They hope the **weather** will be good, too.

When the wheat is ripe, the farmers **harvest**, or gather, it. Long ago many people and animals were needed to harvest the wheat. Today the family needs just two machines. They use machines called combines. Combines cut the wheat. They separate

Farmers like the Hoffmans use a machine called a plow. The plow breaks up the soil to get it ready for planting.

Wheat needs rain and sun to grow. Sometimes after a rainstorm, the Hoffmans can see a rainbow in the sky.

the grain from the straw. They keep the grain and drop the straw on the ground. Long ago, people worked many days to harvest their wheat. Today a combine harvests two acres of wheat in about an hour.

When the wheat turns golden, it is time for the harvest. The Hoffmans use two combines to harvest their wheat.

These foods are made from wheat. Name each food you see.
What other foods are made from wheat?

After the harvest the Hoffmans **sell** their wheat for money. The wheat is used to make foods we eat. Your breakfast cereal may have come from wheat grown on the Hoffman farm. Many people depend on wheat for food.

Checking Up

1. On which landform is this farm located?
2. Why do the Hoffmans sell their wheat?
3. What answers would you give to the key questions at the beginning of this chapter?
4. *Look at the picture on this page. What foods would you miss if farmers could not grow wheat?*

A Dairy Farm in Wisconsin

As You Read

1. Think about these words.
   produce   product
2. Look for answers to these key questions.
   a. Why does this family raise cows?
   b. How do the people in this family help on
      the farm?

The farm in this picture is a dairy farm. It is
located in the hills of Wisconsin. The Baxter family
raises cows. Their cows **produce**, or make, milk.
Some of this milk is used to make milk **products**
such as cheese.

Find the state of
Wisconsin on the map
on pages 12–13. Is it
north, south, east, or
west of where you live?

49

Mr. and Mrs. Baxter milk their cows twice a day. Look at these pictures. What is happening in each picture?

Dairy Farming Long Ago

Many years ago, Mr. Baxter's grandparents owned the dairy farm. There were no machines to help them milk their cows. They milked the cows by hand. Dairy farming has changed a lot since then. It used to take about two hours to milk seventeen cows. Today, with machines, the Baxters can milk about sixty cows in two hours.

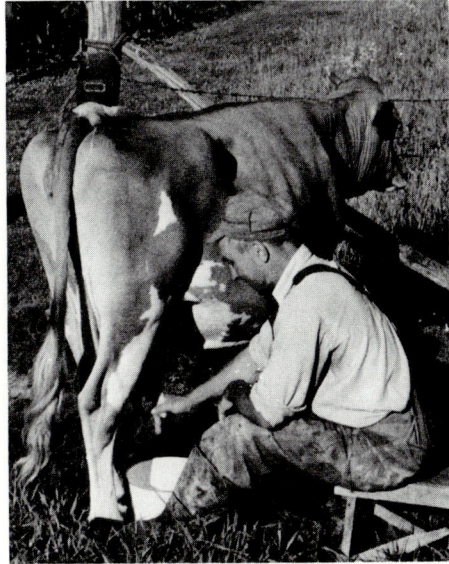

Milk is the only food the Baxters produce to sell. However, the Baxters produce other foods for their own use. They raise chickens and have a large vegetable garden. They go to the store for some of the food they need, but they use their own milk, vegetables, chickens, and eggs.

Look at these pictures. What jobs do the Baxter children have on the farm?

51

Which of these dairy products does your family use? What other dairy products can you think of?

The Baxters depend on their cows to produce enough milk to sell. They sell the milk to the dairy. The Baxters use the money from the milk they sell.

The dairy packages milk for stores to sell. The dairy also makes other milk products. Name the milk products in the picture above.

Many people depend on dairy farms.

Checking Up
1. Name four milk products.
2. What answers would you give to the key questions at the beginning of this chapter?
3. *Why are dairy farms important to us?*

A Rice Farm in Texas

As You Read

1. Think about this word.
   irrigate
2. Look for answers to these key questions.
   a. How is rice like wheat?
   b. How do farmers grow rice?

Look at this picture of a rice farm. Rice is very much like wheat. Both of these crops are grains. Both are grown on plains. Rice and wheat are different, too. Rice grows in fields filled with water.

Mr. and Mrs. Garcia own this rice farm. They live in Texas near the Gulf of Mexico. The weather in this location is hot and wet. The summer is long. The Garcias grow rice because it grows well in hot and wet places.

Find the state of Texas on the map on pages 12–13.

The Garcias produce a lot of rice. However, they do not need a lot of people working on their farm. The Garcias use machines to help them.

Like many other Texas rice farmers, the Garcias plant their rice in an interesting way. First, they soak rice seeds in water for about two days. Then an airplane flies over the fields and drops the rice seeds. Next, the Garcias turn on the water pipes to **irrigate** the fields. They need this water to flood the fields. The rice will begin to grow underwater. The Garcias will irrigate the rice fields all summer.

Using an airplane to scatter seeds over their fields, the Garcias can plant rice quickly.

A pumping station pumps water through the pipes and onto the Garcias' fields.

Rice farmers provide us with products like white rice, brown rice, rice flour, rice pudding, and rice cookies.

At the end of the summer, a cluster of rice hangs from each stalk.

When the grain turns golden, it is time to harvest it. First, the Garcias drain the fields. The Garcias use combines to harvest the rice. The combines cut the stalks and keep the grain. They leave the stalks on the ground and empty the grain into a truck.

Like the other farmers, the Garcias sell their rice. Rice is used in many ways. The rice from their farm helps feed many people.

Checking Up

1. Why is this Texas location good for growing rice?
2. What answers would you give to the key questions at the beginning of this chapter?
3. *In what way is growing rice different from growing wheat?*

Maps Tell a Story of Location

As you read, think about this word.

location

In this unit you have read about three farms in the United States. The farms were the same in some ways, but they were also different. One thing that made them different was the **location**, or where they were.

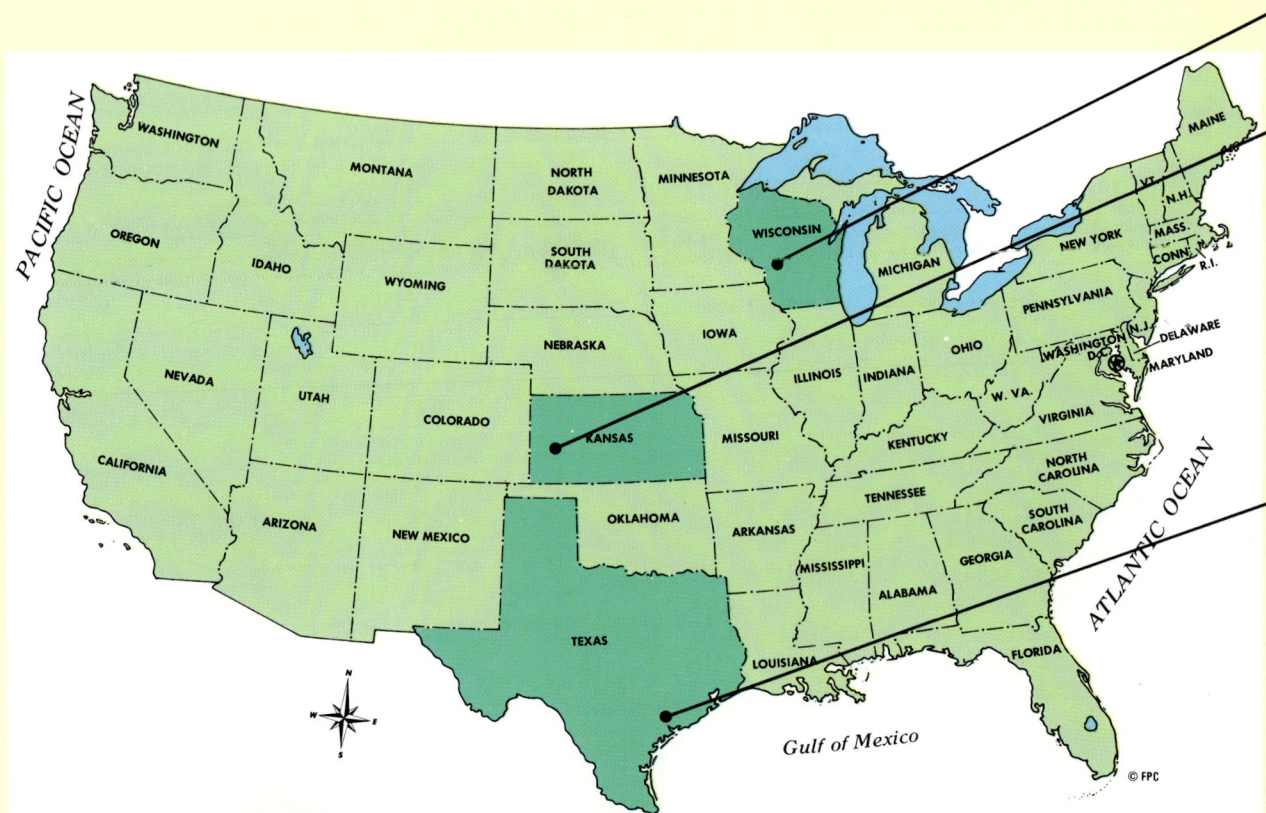

Look at this map of the United States. The pictures show you the location of each farm.

1. Name the state where each farm is found.
2. Which of these states is farthest north?
3. Which of these states is farthest south?
4. Which of these states is almost in the middle of our country?

A Rice Farm in Java

As You Read

1. Think about this word.

   terrace

2. Look for answers to these key questions.

   a. Why is rice important to this family?

   b. This farm grows rice on what kind of land?

3. Use this reading skill.

   As you read this chapter, think about the rice farm in Texas. How are the two farms the same? How are they different? What can you tell about both farms by looking at the pictures?

The farm on the next page does not look like the farm in Texas. Still, the two farms are alike. They both grow rice. This farm is a long way from Texas. It is on the island of Java. There are rice farms in Texas and in Java because rice grows well in both locations.

Rice grows in hot and wet places. Texas is hot and wet part of the time. The Garcias can grow only one crop a year. Java is hot and wet all the time. The Sutomos can grow two crops of rice each year.

Most farm families in Java do not grow rice to sell. They eat what they grow. Rice is their most important food. Everyone helps on this rice farm.

The Sutomos and many other rice farmers in Java grow their rice on mountains. The farmers build **terraces**, or steps, on the slopes of these mountains. Rain collects on the terraces and keeps them flooded.

Java is far away from the other places we have studied so far. Find Java on the map on pages 8–9.

Farm families plant rice seeds in a seedbed. They cover the seeds with soft mud.

Water buffalo pull a plow through the fields. This prepares the soil for planting.

Families lift the young rice plants out of the seedbed and plant them in the fields by hand.

Farm families use knives to cut down the rice plants. Here many people help one family harvest rice.

These pictures show how farm families in Java grow the rice they need. Their work provides food for their families.

Sometimes the Sutomos have extra rice to sell at the market. With the rice money, they can buy other things like vegetables and clothing.

The Sutomo family sits down to a meal of rice and vegetables.

Checking Up

1. Why can rice grow in both Texas and Java?
2. What answers would you give to the key questions at the beginning of this chapter?
3. *How are the two rice farms the same? How are they different?*

A Farm Village in China

As You Read

1. Think about this word.
   village
2. Look for the answer to this key question.
   How is this farm different from all the other farms in this unit?

This picture shows a very large tea farm. It is located in southern China. The tea farm is different from the other farms we have read about. Many families work on this farm. Their homes are in a **village**, or small community.

A young woman uses a tool called a hoe to smooth the soil around the young tea bushes.

The Lin family is like other families on this tea farm. They spend most of their time working in the village tea fields.

Workers plant seeds in seedbeds. In about a year, the seeds grow into small bushes. Then workers plant the bushes in the fields. Three to five years later, the tea is ready to harvest.

Tea leaves must be picked from the plant by hand. The village farmers work together to grow tea.

At the harvest each worker picks as much as forty pounds of tea each day. Many people in China drink tea.

While Mr. and Mrs. Lin work in the fields, their children go to school with other children.

Many people around the world drink tea.

Checking Up

1. Describe this farm village.
2. What answer would you give to the key question at the beginning of this chapter?
3. *How would living on this tea farm be different from living on the wheat farm? How would it be the same?*

Unit 2 Summary

- There are many different kinds of farms around the world.
- Some farmers use machines. Some do not.
- Location often helps the farmer decide what to produce.
- Many people depend on farm products for food, clothing, and shelter.

Graphs Tell a Story of Weather

As you read, think about these words.

weather   rainfall   temperature

People often talk about the **weather**. Weather describes what it is like outside. Sometimes the weather is hot. Other times it is cold. Sometimes we have rainy weather. Rain is important to us. How does rain help us?

Measuring Rainfall

Because rain is important, we measure it to find out how much rain has fallen. We measure **rainfall** in inches.

Look at the graph on page 66. This graph shows the number of inches of rainfall each farm received during the year. Find the numbers on the graph. These numbers show inches of rainfall. On the left side of the graph are the names of the different farms you have studied. The blue bars show how much rain fell on each farm in one year. For example, find the wheat farm. Look at the blue bar. It is colored up to the line marked 30. That means that this farm had 30 inches of rain in one year.

Rain Bar Graph

	0	10	20	30	40	50	60	70	80	90
Kansas Wheat Farm	███████████									
Wisconsin Dairy Farm	███████████									
Texas Rice Farm	██████████████████									
Java Rice Farm	█████████████████████████████									
China Tea Farm	██████████████████									

Inches of rain each year

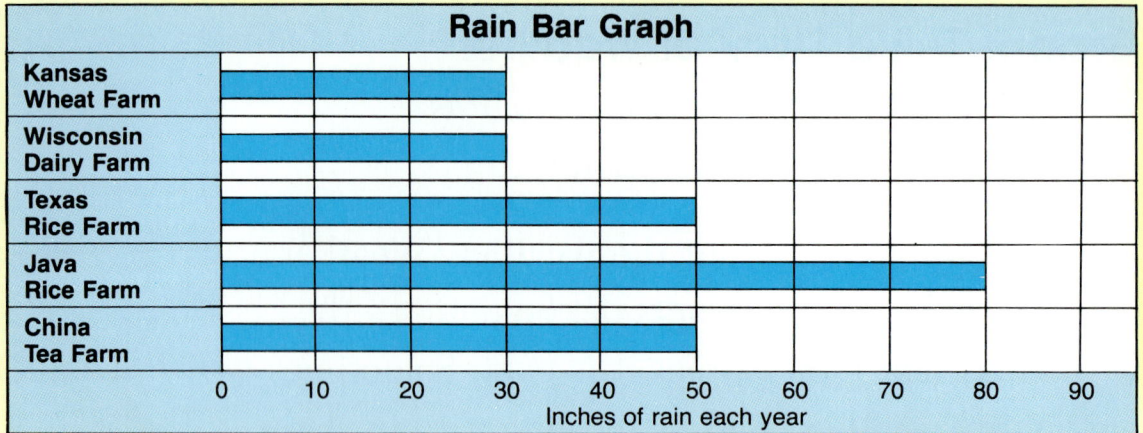

1. How many inches of rain did each of the other farms have?
2. Which farm had the most rainfall?
3. Which farms had the least rainfall?
4. Which farms received the same amount?

Measuring Temperature

We often talk about warm or cold weather. The **temperature** tells us just how warm or cold the weather is. Temperature is very important to farmers. They need to know if the temperature will be right for the crops they grow.

Temperature is measured by a thermometer. Look at the picture on the right. The higher the red line on the thermometer goes, the warmer the temperature. The lower the red line goes, the cooler the temperature.

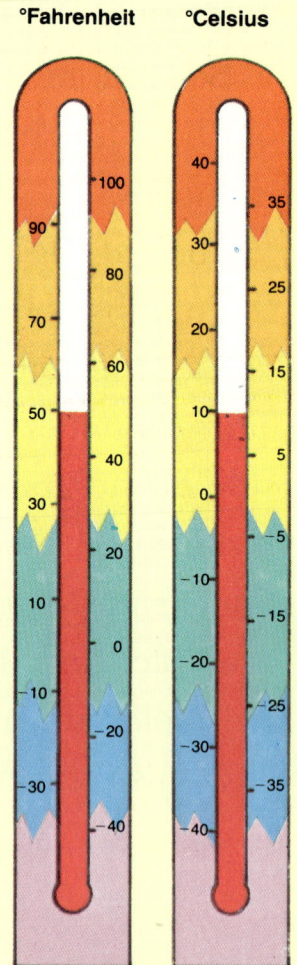

°Fahrenheit   °Celsius

66

Temperature Bar Graph

Color Key = January   = July

°F

°C

80 ——— 27

70 ——— 21

60 ——— 16

50 ——— 10

Temperature

40 ——— 4

30 ——— −1

20 ——— −7

10 ——— −12

Temperature

Jan. July   Jan. July   Jan. July   Jan. July   Jan. July
Kansas   **Wisconsin** **Texas**   **Java**   **China**
Wheat Farm **Dairy Farm** **Rice Farm** **Rice Farm** **Tea Farm**

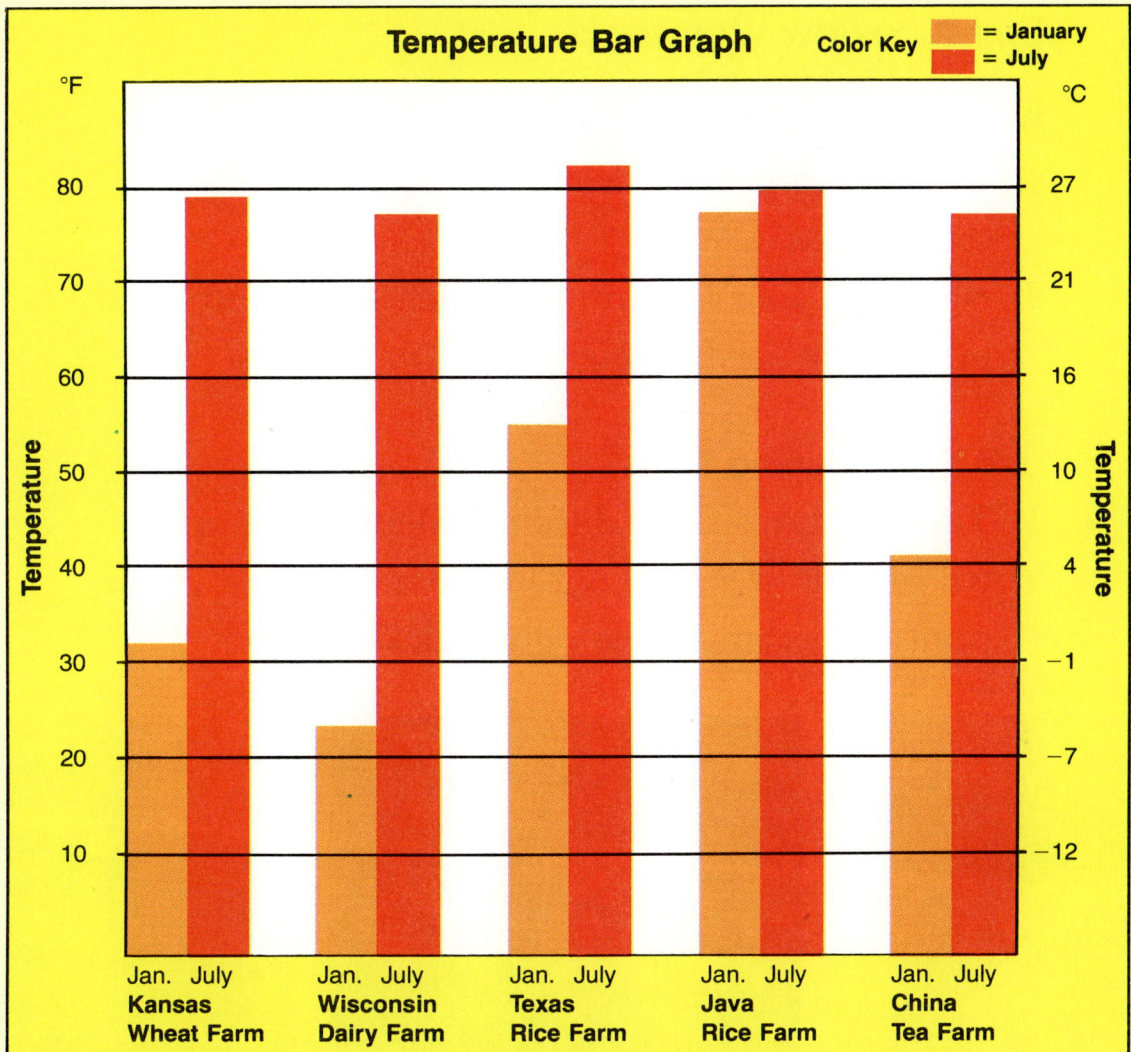

Now look at the graph on this page. It shows the temperature for each farm in this unit. It shows the temperatures for two months, January and July.

1. Which farm is the coolest in January?
2. Which farm is the warmest in January?
3. Which farm is the warmest in July?
4. On which farm is the temperature almost the same in January as in July?

Unit 2 Review Workshop

What Have You Learned?

1. Farms help people meet important needs. Name these needs.

2. Name the four landforms. Which three were used in this unit for farming?

Use Your Reading Skills

1. These pictures show different steps for growing wheat. The steps are out of order. On your paper, print the letters in the right order.

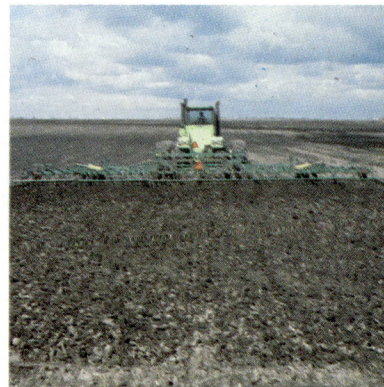

A   B   C

2. In this unit you read about wheat, dairy, rice, and tea farms. Look at the pictures on pages 41–43. Some of these pictures show other kinds of farms and farm products. List at least four. Which of these farms provide products your family uses?

Use Your Thinking Skills

1. Look at the pictures above. If you were going to become a rice farmer, which of these places would you pick for your farm? Why?
2. Why would the other two places not be good?

Learn by Doing

The next time someone in your family goes to the store, go along. Take a pencil and a piece of paper. List products that wheat farms and dairy farms help produce.

Unit 3

People Live in Towns

In the fall, trees with leaves of many colors surround this small town in Vermont.

Towns Are Communities

As You Read

1. Think about these words.
   community   goods   services   natural resource
2. Look for answers to these key questions.
   a. How are towns alike?
   b. How are they different?
   c. What are natural resources?

You know that some people live on farms. Other people live in **communities**. In communities people live near one another. Communities are located in many places around the world.

Communities can be different sizes. A small community is usually called a town. There are more people in a town than on a farm.

Towns are alike in many ways. There are homes for people. There are places for people to buy and sell **goods**. Goods are things that people grow, raise, or make. Towns also have **services** for people. Services help people. Some people who provide services are doctors, teachers, and community workers.

Many people depend on the goods and services in towns. Look at the pictures below. What goods or services are these people providing?

What are other ways that people in towns help one another?

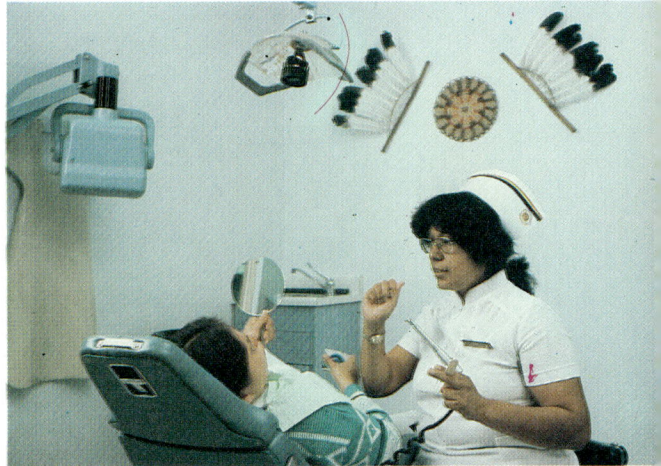

Coal miners dig for coal underground. Coal is an important natural resource used for fuel.

Towns are alike, but they are also different. Their locations are different. Some towns are near oceans, lakes, or rivers. Some are in mountains or on hills. Still others are on plains or plateaus.

Towns are also different because of the **natural resources** around them. Natural resources are things in or on the earth that people use. Land, trees, and water are three natural resources. In some towns workers use natural resources to provide things that people need and want.

Fish are also a natural resource. This town is located near water. It provides many fishing jobs for people in the town.

There are many kinds of towns. In some ways they are the same. In other ways they are different.

Checking Up

1. Name two kinds of goods that people in towns provide.
2. Name four services that people in towns often provide.
3. What answers would you give to the key questions at the beginning of this chapter?
4. *How do you think living in a town is different from living on a farm?*

A Community for Farmers

As You Read

1. Think about these words.
   service center
2. Look for answers to these key questions.
   a. How do farm families depend on the town?
   b. How do the town's people depend on the farmers?

Look at the picture below. This is a town in Iowa. Find Iowa on the Atlas map on pages 12–13. Iowa is in a plains area. The land is flat and good for farming. The map on page 28 shows the plain where Iowa is located.

There are farms all around the town. The Johnson family owns one of the farms. Their farm does not produce everything they need or want. They depend on nearby towns for many things. The people in this town provide many goods and services for people on farms and in town. This town is a **service center** for them.

In town the Johnsons can store or sell the corn from their farm. There is also a bank where they can keep their money. They buy food and clothing in the town. Sometimes the Johnsons go to doctors and dentists in the town.

After they harvest their corn, the Johnsons take the corn to the grain elevator in town.

There are several different kinds of stores in town. Here the Johnsons shop in a sporting goods store.

Look at the pictures below. What are some of the other services in town?

The Johnson children depend on the town to provide them with a place to go to school.

The children belong to a club for young people. It is called 4–H. Often the club has meetings in town.

The town has a library. At the library the Johnsons can check out books they want to read.

What places can you find in this town? How is it
like your community?

The people who own this restaurant in town depend on farm families and families in town to give them business.

Farm families like the Johnsons need the goods and services provided by the people in the service center. People in the town need the farm families to provide them with jobs.

Checking Up

1. Why do we call towns service centers?
2. What answers would you give to the key questions at the beginning of this chapter?
3. *Which do you think came first, the farms or the town?*

A Market Community

As You Read

1. Think about these words.
   market community
2. Look for answers to this key question.
   Why do the Kims come to the market community?

In some places small towns are called villages. The community on page 82 is a village in the mountains of Guatemala. Guatemala is a country in Central America. Central America is just north and west of South America. Find Central America on the Atlas map on pages 8–9. What country is just north and west of Guatemala?

Indian families live in the mountains around the village. They farm on small pieces of land. The Kim family lives there. Like the Johnsons in Iowa, the Kims need a place where they can buy food they do not grow. They need a place to buy other goods besides food. The Kims also need a place to sell some of their own crops. The village market provides them with a place to buy and sell food and other goods. This village is a **market community**.

Farm families from the mountains come into the village. They bring goods they have made and part of the crops they have grown. The farm families hope to sell what they have brought to the market community.

People come to the market village to buy and sell food and other goods, such as baskets, pots, and cloth.

The market community also provides the Kims with a place to meet and talk with friends.

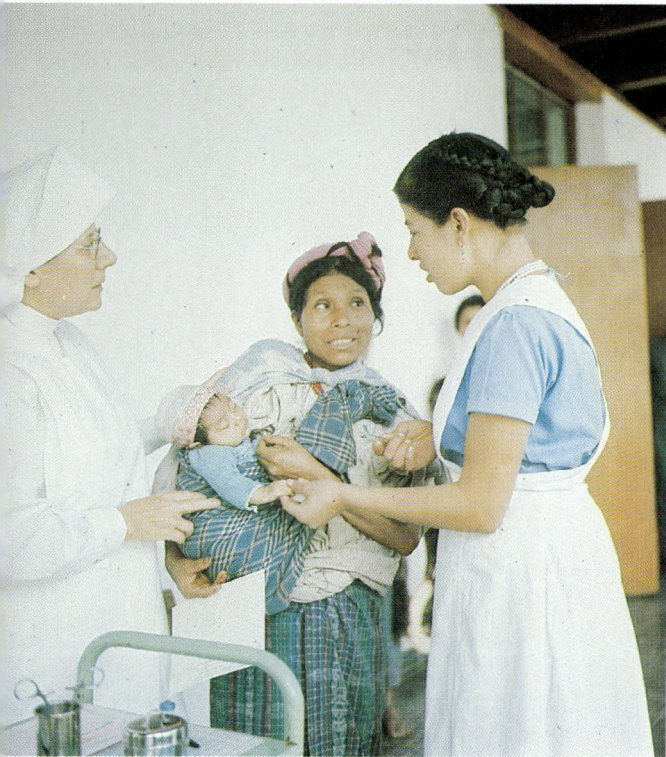

The market community provides other things. Sometimes when the Kims come to town, they go to the doctor.

The people who come to the market community depend on one another. They sell their crops and other goods to one another. They will use the money they make to buy other things.

Checking Up

1. How do these families depend on one another?
2. What answers would you give to the key question at the beginning of this chapter?
3. *How are the market community and the farm community in Iowa alike? How are they different?*

A Recreation Community

As You Read

1. Think about these words.

   recreation   recreation community
2. Look for the answer to this key question.
   Why does this community provide goods and
   services to people from other communities?
3. Use this reading skill.
   As you read this chapter, decide which sentence
   below best describes the recreation community.

   a. This community provides recreation, goods,
      and services to many people.

   b. People come to this community to give the
      town the money it needs.

Carol Russo is in the third grade. Each morning
she walks up the hill to her school. On her way she
sees many people along the street. The people are
having a good time. They are going into restaurants
for breakfast. Some are on their way to ski. Others
are looking at gift shops. Still others are riding
horses. These people do not live in this town. They
are on vacation.

Carol lives in a town in Colorado. Find Colorado on the Atlas map on pages 12–13. This town is located in the Rocky Mountains. You can see these mountain areas on the map on pages 8–9. In winter the mountains are covered with snow. People come from all over the United States to ski. Many people also enjoy the mountains in the summer. Sometimes people call having fun **recreation**. This town is a **recreation community**. The mountains provide many kinds of recreation for many people.

Mr. Russo works in the post office. People who spend their vacations in this town depend on his services. Before they come for vacation, they write the hotels to reserve rooms. Mrs. Russo works in one of these hotels. Without workers like Mr. and Mrs. Russo, people could not plan their vacations.

What other services might the people of this town provide for the vacationers?

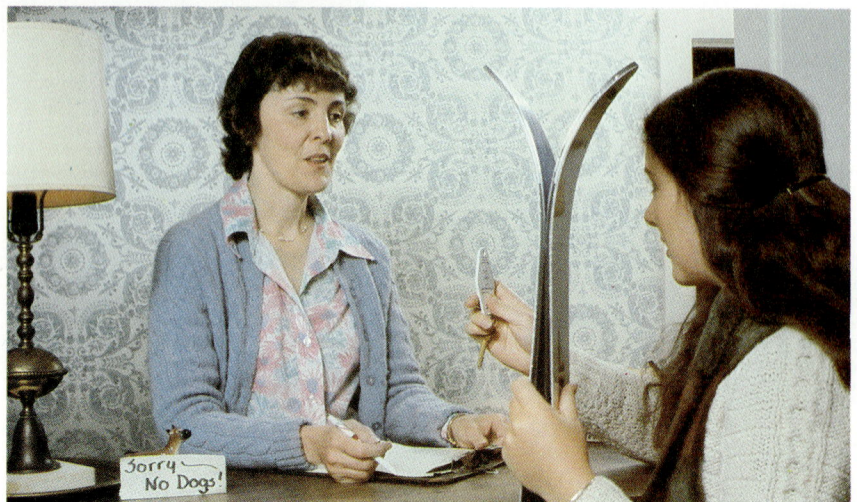

The people of this recreation community know
that their services are important. By providing
services for vacationers, many people in the town
earn money. Then they use this money to buy the
things they need and want.

Checking Up

1. How does this community depend on its location?
2. What answer would you give to the key question
   at the beginning of this chapter?
3. *Why do you think people like the Russos moved
   to this community?*

A Logging Community

The Nightwalkers live in a town in the state of Washington. Find the state of Washington on the Atlas map on pages 12–13. Their town is at the foot of a mountain range. The mountains are covered with forests. The many trees in the forests are a natural resource. Trees are used for wood, or **lumber**. Mr. Nightwalker and many other people in this town are **loggers**. Loggers are workers who cut down trees for lumber. This town is a **logging community**. Workers in logging communities produce lumber for homes and other buildings.

Many years ago a lumber company came to the town. People knew the company would do well in this location near the forests. The company provided jobs for many people. More people came to the town to work for the lumber company. The town grew. The company grew. Today many people in the town depend on the forests for their jobs.

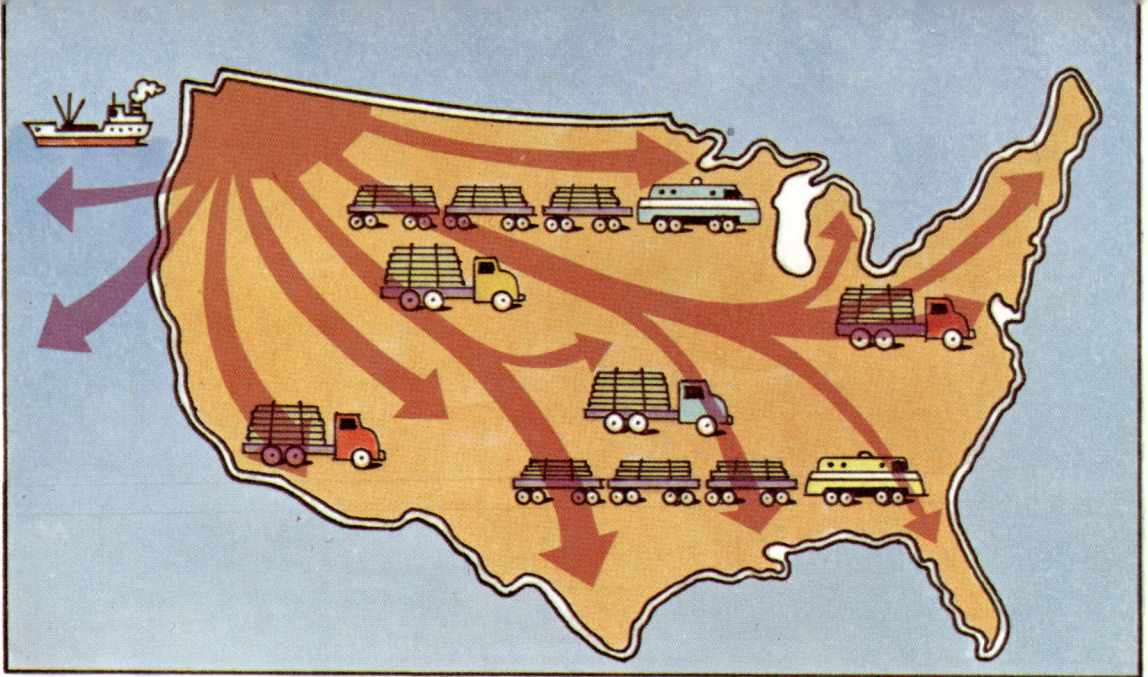

Trucks, trains, and ships carry lumber from logging communities like this one to many different locations.

Not everyone in the logging community works for the lumber company. As in other communities, some people work in food and clothing stores. Some work in the bank. Some are teachers and doctors. Other people are fire fighters. People who work for the lumber company need these goods and services. People who provide these goods and services need the loggers, too.

Bank workers, store owners, and many other people who provide services depend on the loggers for business.

How Wood Is Made into Paper

Lumber is the main product that comes from trees. Lumber is used to make buildings, crates, furniture, boats, and many other products people use every day.

Did you know that other products are also made from trees? One of these products is paper. Most paper is made from tree logs or small pieces of wood not used by lumber companies. Wood goes through many steps to become paper.

Wood is cut into chips.

Chips are cooked and made into pulp.

Air blows on the pulp and makes it fluffy.

The pulp is pressed flat. Water is squeezed out.

Steamrollers help thin and dry the paper.

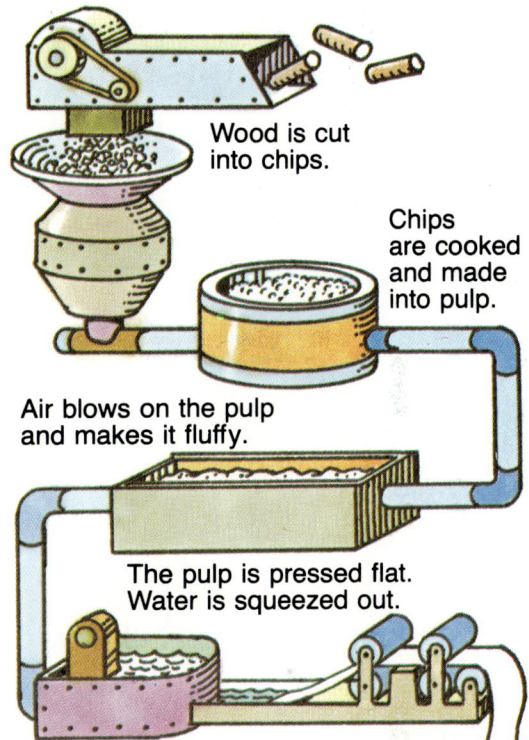

Checking Up

1. How is this community important to other communities?
2. What answers would you give to the key question at the beginning of this chapter?
3. *Look at the picture of this town on page 88. Is this community larger or smaller than where you live?*

Maps Tell a Story of Direction and Location

As you read, think about these words.

in-between direction   compass rose

compass   symbol

Direction

You already know about the four main directions: north, south, east, and west. Sometimes places are located in between main directions. For example, what if you wanted to go to a place that was located between north and west? You would go northwest. Northwest is an **in-between direction**. In-between directions are halfway between the main directions.

There are four in-between directions. They are northeast, southeast, southwest, and northwest. Look at the Atlas map on pages 12–13. If you were in Kansas, in what direction would you travel to go to the state of Washington? In what direction would you travel to go to Florida?

Rick wanted to make a map of his town. To begin drawing his map, he wanted to find north. He used his **compass**. A compass is a tool that shows direction. Its needle always points north, toward the North Pole. Then Rick drew a **compass rose** on his map. A compass rose shows directions on a map. Find the compass rose on Rick's map on page 94.

Symbols and Location

Maps can show many things. They can show land and water. They can also show things people put on the land.

Many maps use small drawings to show us things. These drawings, or **symbols**, stand for something on the land. A map key shows what these symbols mean. Rick used symbols to show things in and around his town. Study his map key on page 94 to help you learn about his town. Find each symbol on the map. Use the symbols and directions to answer questions about this map.

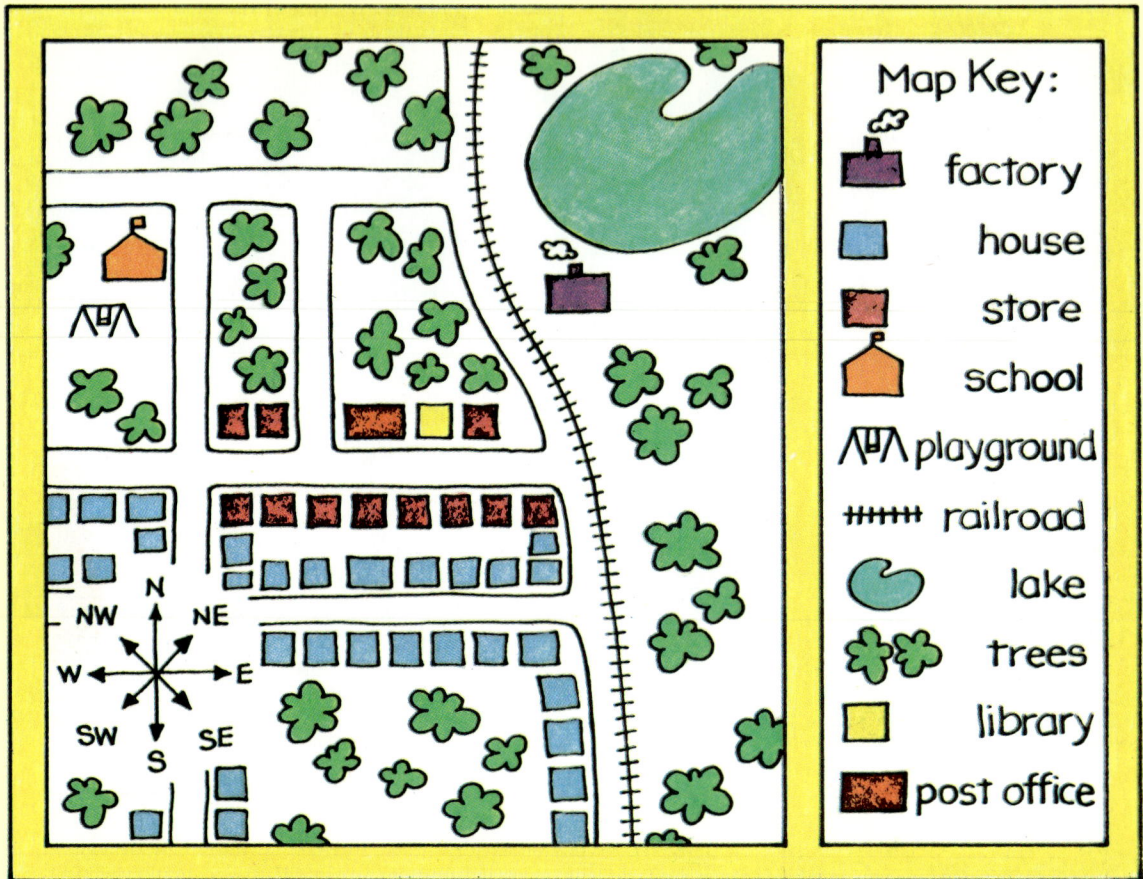

1. Which building is the farthest north?
2. Charles, Rick's friend, lives near the railroad tracks. In what direction is the school from his house?
3. Rick lives in the southwest part of town. The library is in what direction from his house?
4. In what direction will Rick go to get from the town to the lake?
5. Look at the Atlas map on pages 12–13. In what direction would you travel to get from your state to Washington, D.C.?

A Manufacturing Community

As You Read

1. Think about these words.
   manufacture   manufacturing community
   textile
2. Look for the answer to this key question.
   How do other people depend on the people of
   this community?

Look at the picture on this page. This town is
located in North Carolina. North Carolina is located
along the east coast of the United States. Find North
Carolina on your Atlas map on pages 12–13.

Many towns in our country provide us with important products. Some products are **manufactured**, or made, in factories.

This town is a **manufacturing community**. It produces yarn used to make cloth, or **textiles**. Textiles are used to make clothes, curtains, and other products people need and want.

The Wallace family lives in this town. Mrs. Wallace works for a textile company. She tests dyes to color the yarn. Many people in this town depend on the textile company for jobs. The company depends on people like Mrs. Wallace. She helps produce a product that the company can sell.

The people in manufacturing communities make products. Different communities make different kinds of products. People all around the world depend on products from manufacturing communities.

Mrs. Wallace works with other people to test new colors for yarn.

Inside the factory people take the yarn and make it into cloth. The cloth is then made into products we use every day.

Checking Up

1. What is a manufacturing community?
2. What answer would you give to the key question at the beginning of this chapter?
3. *How is this community like your community? How is it different?*

Unit 3 Summary

- A community is a place where people live near one another.
- Communities are different sizes.
- One kind of community is a town. There are many different kinds of towns.
- The people of a town provide goods and services for one another. They depend on their community and on other communities.

Unit 3 Review Workshop

What Have You Learned?

1. Name five things that a town can provide for its people.
2. Which two communities provide important products to people in other communities?
3. To which two communities do farmers go to get the goods and services they need and want?
4. What is a service center?

Use Your Reading Skills

Towns are alike in many ways. Look at the pictures in this unit. Find pictures that show how each sentence below is true. List the page numbers where these pictures can be found.

1. Towns are places where people buy and sell goods.
2. Towns provide services.
3. Towns are places where people meet with friends.

Use Your Thinking Skills

In this unit you learned about two special kinds of products. People take one of these kinds of products from natural resources. They manufacture other kinds of products in factories. The pictures on page 99 show both kinds of products.

Yarn for textiles

Clothes made from textiles

Lumber

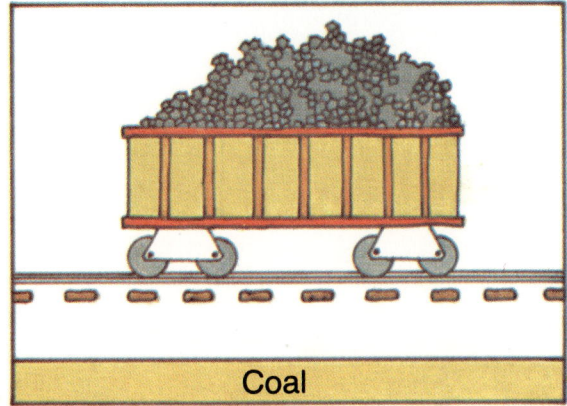
Coal

On your own paper write these two headings:

Products Manufactured in Factories
Products Taken from Natural Resources

Write the names of the products you see in the pictures under the correct headings on your paper.

Learn by Doing

Have a class meeting. Choose a person in your community who provides a service. With the help of your teacher, make plans to have this person visit your class to talk about the service he or she provides.

Unit 4

People Live in Cities

Chicago is a large city located on the shores of Lake Michigan.

Cities Are Communities

As You Read

1. Think about this word.
   population

2. Look for answers to these key questions.
   a. How are towns and cities alike?
   b. How are they different?

3. Use this reading skill.
   In this unit you will find some sentences that ask you to do something important. You might be asked to look at pictures and answer questions about the pictures. You might be asked to turn to another page and study a map. This is called following directions. Following directions helps you understand more about what you read. Make sure that you follow all directions.

Some people live in small communities called towns. People also live in larger communities called cities. The **population** of a city is larger than the population of a town. Population is the number of people living in a place.

Cities and towns are alike in some ways. In both, people live near one another. Both have places for people to get things they need and want. Because the populations of cities are larger, there are more places to get goods and services. There are more stores, office buildings, restaurants, and places to live.

Compare the picture on page 79 with the picture below. How are they alike? How are they different?

The main difference between towns and cities is size. Cities usually cover more land than towns. They need more space for the many people and buildings. Look at the pictures below. Which one shows a city? How can you tell?

Checking Up
1. Which kind of community provides more goods and services, a town or a city?
2. What answers would you give to the key questions at the beginning of this chapter?
3. *Which kind of community needs more roads, a town or a city? Why?*

Maps Tell a Story of Distance and Scale

As you read, think about these words.

distance   map scale

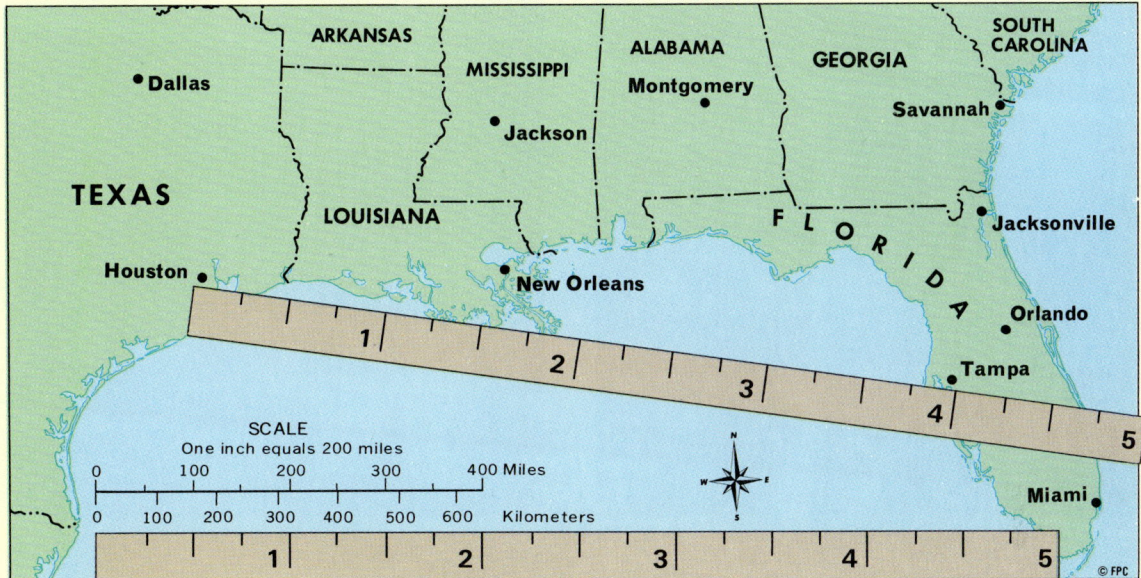

SCALE
One inch equals 200 miles

You can learn many things from maps. You can learn about landforms, location, and direction. You can also learn how to measure **distances** on a map, or how far it is from one place to another. To measure distances shown on a map, you must understand the **map scale**, or the size of the place the map shows.

Pretend you are in a rocket taking off from Cape Canaveral, Florida. A few minutes after you lift off, you take a picture with your camera. Look at picture A on page 106.

Picture A

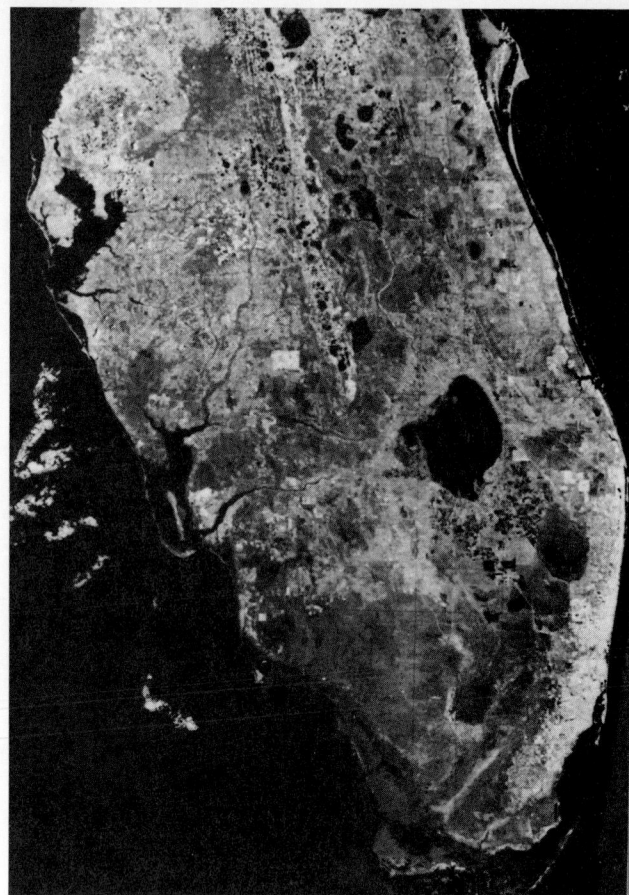

Picture B

The rocket climbs higher into the sky. You take another picture. Look at picture B on page 106. This picture looks different from the first one. You can see more because you are farther away.

After you return to Earth, maps are made from your pictures. Map A on page 107 stands for picture A. Map B stands for picture B.

Map A and map B are the same size. Map A shows only a small part of Florida. It shows the part around Cape Canaveral. Map B shows more than half the state of Florida. Which map shows the most detail? Which map shows the larger area?

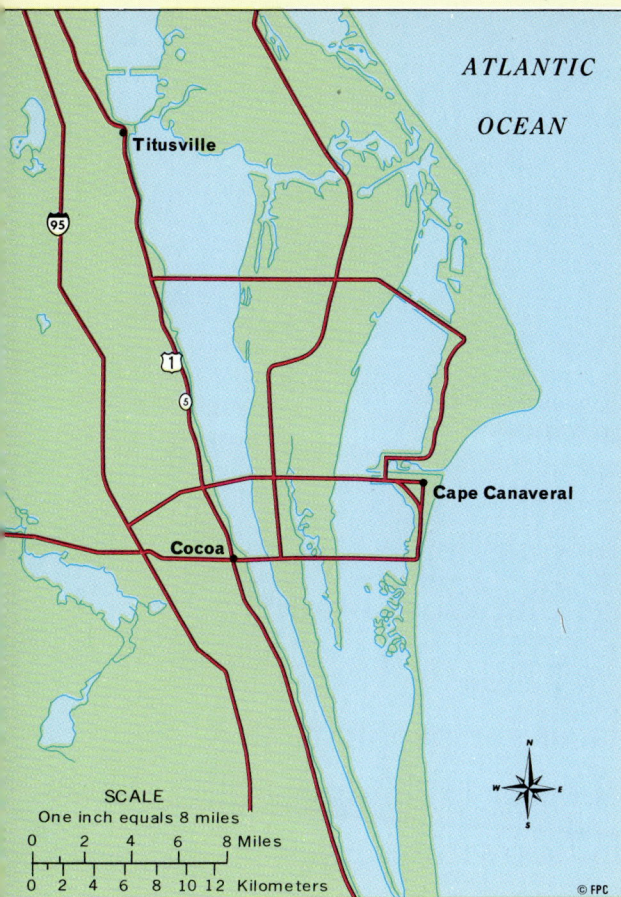

Map A

Map B

Look at map A. In the bottom left-hand corner is the map scale. How many miles does one inch cover on this map? Now find the map scale on map B. How many miles does one inch cover on this map?

Map scales help you measure distances between cities and other places shown on maps. Use the map scales for maps A and B and a ruler to answer these questions.

1. How far is it from Cape Canaveral to Cocoa?
2. How far is it from the city of Tampa to the city of West Palm Beach?
3. How far is it from Orlando to Cape Canaveral?

107

Living in Cities

As You Read

1. Think about these words.
   neighborhood   transportation
   trade   communication
2. Look for answers to this key question.
   What are some of the things that cities offer?

There are many kinds of places for people to live in cities. There are houses and other buildings of all sizes. There are small communities within cities called **neighborhoods**. These neighborhoods have places for people to live, work, shop, and have fun.

Some city neighborhoods, like this one, are made up of houses.

Other city neighborhoods are made up of many tall buildings.

There are many places in cities where people can work. Some people work in places that provide services. Others work in factories that produce goods.

This factory is located in a city. Many people work here to produce jet airplanes.

When people buy and sell goods, it is called **trade**. Cities around the world are important centers of trade. People may travel from one city to another to buy and sell goods. People from smaller communities also shop at the many stores and markets in cities.

Cities provide many kinds of **transportation**, or ways to move people and goods from place to place. Many people use city transportation to go to work and to go to school. They use transportation to visit friends and to go shopping.

City buses stop at places along the street to pick up people. Subway trains go underground and can carry many people.

Some people who work in cities do not live in cities. They use trains and other transportation to bring them to and from work.

Other kinds of transportation carry food and other goods in and out of cities. People and cities depend on transportation.

Trucks deliver food and other goods to many places in cities.

Cars, cabs, and trucks use city streets and highways.

Most cities have airports. Airplanes carry people and goods in and out of cities.

People everywhere depend on cities to provide them with news. Many radio and television stations are located in cities. Many newspapers are written and printed in cities. When people share news by reading, writing, watching, listening, or speaking, it is called **communication**. Cities offer important communication services to people around the world.

Cities offer many other things to people who live in and around them. There are many places where people can learn. There are all kinds of schools. There are libraries and museums. Cities also provide many kinds of recreation. There are parks where people can play or have a picnic. There are places to listen to music or to see a play.

This family enjoys visiting the animals in their city's zoo.

What service does the city on the left need that the city on the right does not need?

Some cities are very old. Other cities are new. Some cities have more people than others. Some cities use more land than others. Some cities have goods and services that are not needed in other cities. There are many kinds of cities. They are located in many kinds of places. In some ways they are different. In some ways they are the same.

Checking Up

1. How do people in cities depend on transportation?
2. What is trade? How are cities important to trade?
3. What answers would you give to the key question at the beginning of this chapter?
4. *Why do you think communication is so important?*

How Cities Began

As You Read

1. Think about this word.
   wanderer
2. Look for answers to these key questions.
   a. How did people live before there were cities?
   b. Why did people begin to live closer together?

There was a time when there were no cities or towns. People did not stay in one location. They were **wanderers**. They moved from place to place. People looked for places where they could find food and water. When they used up all the food, they moved again.

Many, many years passed. Some people found places where the land provided a good supply of food. There were animals to hunt and fish to catch. There was enough wild grain to last a long time. There was water from nearby rivers or lakes. These people stopped moving from place to place. They made their homes in the special places. Because the special locations provided plenty of food and water, more and more people could live there.

People in these locations began to plant seeds from wild grain. Good soil, warm weather, and plenty of water helped the seeds grow. The people grew their own crops. They no longer depended on wild grain. These people were the first farmers.

In time, the farmers began to grow more food than they needed.

The population of these places grew larger. Some people farmed. Some people had other important jobs, like making baskets, pots, and cloth. Others made tools for hunting and farming. Some people protected the community from enemies. All these people traded their goods and services for food from the farmers. People began to depend on one another for the things they needed and wanted.

Some of these communities became very large. The people of these communities provided more and more goods and services. These communities were the first cities.

Checking Up

1. Why did some people of long ago stop wandering from place to place?
2. Why did some people begin other jobs besides farming?
3. What answers would you give to the key questions at the beginning of this chapter?
4. *What are some other services that people in early cities might have provided as time passed?*

A Look at an Ancient City: Rome

As You Read

1. Think about these words.

   ancient   settlement   valley

2. Look for answers to these key questions.

   a. How did ancient Rome begin?

   b. Why did ancient Rome grow?

3. Use this reading skill.

   The word *preview* means "to see ahead of time."
   Previewing a chapter can help you understand
   what the chapter is about. First, look at the title
   of the chapter. What does it tell you about the
   material you are going to read? Second, see if
   there are other lines in the chapter that appear in
   bold type. These are called headings. In this
   chapter you will find two headings, **Rome Begins**
   and **Rome Changes**. What do these headings tell
   you about the information in this chapter? Write
   down the chapter title and the two headings
   under it. When previewing other chapters, make
   sure you write down the chapter title and any
   other headings included in the chapter.

Some cities began a long time ago. Some of these cities still exist today. They are now very old, or **ancient**, cities.

Rome Begins

Rome, like all ancient cities, began as a small community, or **settlement**. It was located on a hill above the Tiber River. There were six other hills around the settlement. The hills helped protect the people from enemies.

Soon other people came to the area. They built their settlements on the six other hills. More people came. They made their homes in the valleys, or the low land between the hills. Still more people came to the area. After many years the settlements joined together to become the city of Rome.

Look carefully at the map of ancient Rome above. Find the Tiber River. Why was this a good location for the city to begin?

Rome Changes

Many, many years passed. Rome grew and changed. Rome became the largest city in the world. Rome was a crowded and busy city. It was a beautiful city, too.

People met and talked with friends at markets called forums.

Ancient Rome had many theaters where people could see plays.

Like the cities of today, ancient Rome was an important center for transportation. Roads led from Rome to other cities. Ships traveled from Rome to other parts of the world. Many goods produced in Rome were taken to other cities. People from other places traveled to Rome to buy and sell goods. Because of good transportation, Rome became an important center of trade.

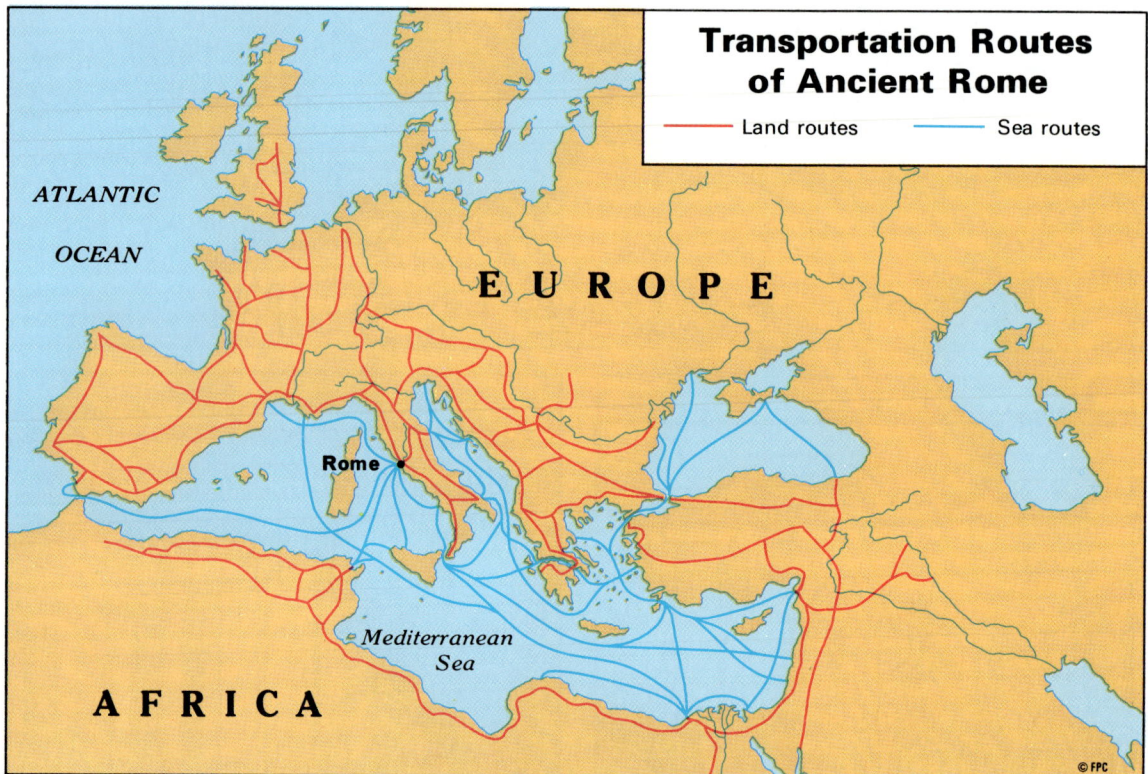

Transportation Routes of Ancient Rome

— Land routes   — Sea routes

ATLANTIC

OCEAN

E U R O P E

Rome

Mediterranean
Sea

A F R I C A

© FPC

The Romans built many roads leading to faraway places. Road and ship routes connected Rome to other settlements in both Europe and Africa.

Today visitors to Rome can still see many of the old forums, theaters, and other buildings.

As the years passed, Rome continued to change. Rome still exists today. It is an ancient and interesting city. Rome is still one of the most important cities in the world.

Checking Up

1. How was transportation important to the people of ancient Rome?
2. Look at the pictures on page 121. Name one way in which communication took place in ancient Rome. Name a kind of recreation in ancient Rome.
3. What answers would you give to the key questions at the beginning of this chapter?
4. *Look again at the pictures of ancient Rome on page 121. Now look at the picture of Rome today on this page. How has it changed?*

Cities of Today

As You Read

1. Think about this word.
   law

2. Look for answers to these key questions.
   a. How have cities changed since the days of ancient Rome?
   b. Why do cities need laws?

Cities have changed since the early days of Rome. Cities are larger. Buildings are taller. More trade takes place in cities than ever before. City transportation has changed. Radio and television have made communication better.

Over many years more and more people have moved to cities. Look at the graph on this page. It shows how city populations have grown. In the year 1920, one out of every ten people in the world lived in cities. How many people out of every ten lived in cities in 1950? in 1980? People who study cities say that most cities will probably keep growing.

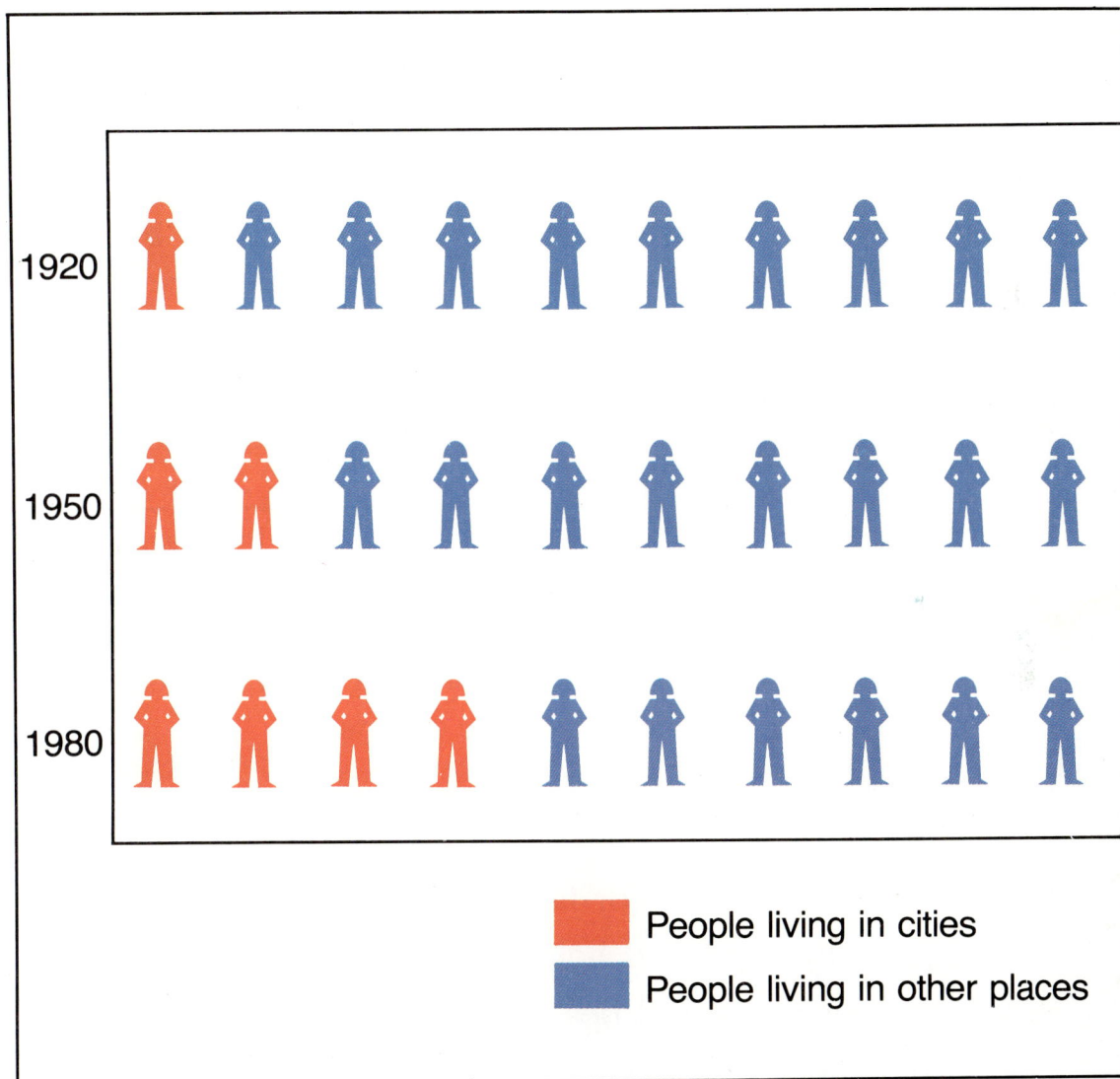

1920

1950

1980

■ People living in cities

■ People living in other places

How Laws Are Made

People choose community leaders, or lawmakers, who they think will work hard to solve problems of their areas of the city. These lawmakers listen to people tell about the changes they would like to see in their city.

Lawmakers from around the city hold meetings with the mayor. They talk about the changes people would like to see in their city. They discuss what laws need to be made to keep the city safe for everyone. Lawmakers vote to decide if a new law needs to be made or if an old law needs to be changed.

All cities need rules, or **laws**. Laws make cities safe for everyone. Laws help keep cities and other communities clean and beautiful. What laws can you name that help the people of your community?

It is important that all people obey laws. Laws help make cities and other communities good places to live.

Checking Up

1. Write three sentences that describe cities of today.
2. What answers would you give to the key questions at the beginning of this chapter?
3. *Why do you think laws are important? Name a law that you think most cities would have for their people to obey.*

Unit 4 Summary

- Cities have larger populations than towns have.
- Cities provide many goods and services for many people.
- Cities are centers for transportation, trade, communication, and recreation.
- The first cities began many, many years ago.
- Rome was an ancient city that still exists today.
- Today more and more people are moving to cities.
- Cities and other communities have laws that help keep people safe.

Unit 4 Review Workshop

What Have You Learned?

1. Which kind of community needs more fire fighters, a town or a city?
2. Name three ways in which most cities are alike.
3. How did the first cities begin?
4. Name three ways in which the cities of today are like ancient Rome.

Use Your Reading Skills

Eight new social studies words that you learned in this unit are listed here. Match each of these words with its correct meaning below.

valley	distance	communication
trade	law	transportation
wanderer	population	

1. How far it is from one place to another
2. Reading, writing, watching, listening, or speaking
3. The number of people living in a place
4. A rule
5. Ways for people and goods to move from place to place
6. Low land between hills
7. The buying and selling of goods
8. A person who moves from place to place

Use Your Group Skills

Form a group with two or three other people in your class. Choose one person to write down the group's ideas. Next, as a group, make a list of at least ten people, places, and things that you find in the city pictured above. Then decide which seven items on your list are most important to all cities. Discuss reasons for your choices. Share your seven choices with other groups in the class. Are your group's choices the same as the choices made by other groups? Why or why not?

Learn by Doing

Think of a law that helps keep your community safe or clean. Make a poster that shows how people should obey this law.

Unit 5

Cities Grow

Los Angeles, California, is a large, growing city.

Los Angeles Begins

As You Read

1. Think about these words.
   explorer   mission
2. Look for the answer to this key question.
   What was Los Angeles like when it first began?
3. Use these reading skills.
   In this book you have learned how to use many reading skills. Some of these skills are how to use the Glossary, how to "read" pictures, how to follow directions, and how to preview a chapter. As you continue to read this book, practice each skill. Use these reading skills even when you are not told to use them. Practicing these reading skills on your own will make you a better reader.

Some cities are very large. They have large populations and cover a lot of land. These large cities were not always large. They grew because people wanted to live and work in them.

Look at the picture on page 131. It is of Los Angeles, California. Los Angeles is a very large city in the United States. It is a city that grew and that keeps growing. Use the Atlas map on pages 12–13

to find Los Angeles. How would you describe
its location?

Many years ago the land where Los Angeles is
located looked different. There were no stores or
tall buildings. There were no streets or highways.
The land was covered with grass and trees. Small
groups of American Indians lived near the river
that flowed through the area.

What natural resources of the area did the Indians use? Where
did their food come from? How did the river help them?

This location was a good place to live. The land was a plain. To the north and east were mountains. To the west was the ocean. The mountains and ocean protected the plain and helped make the weather mild. It was cool in the summer, and it did not get very cold in the winter.

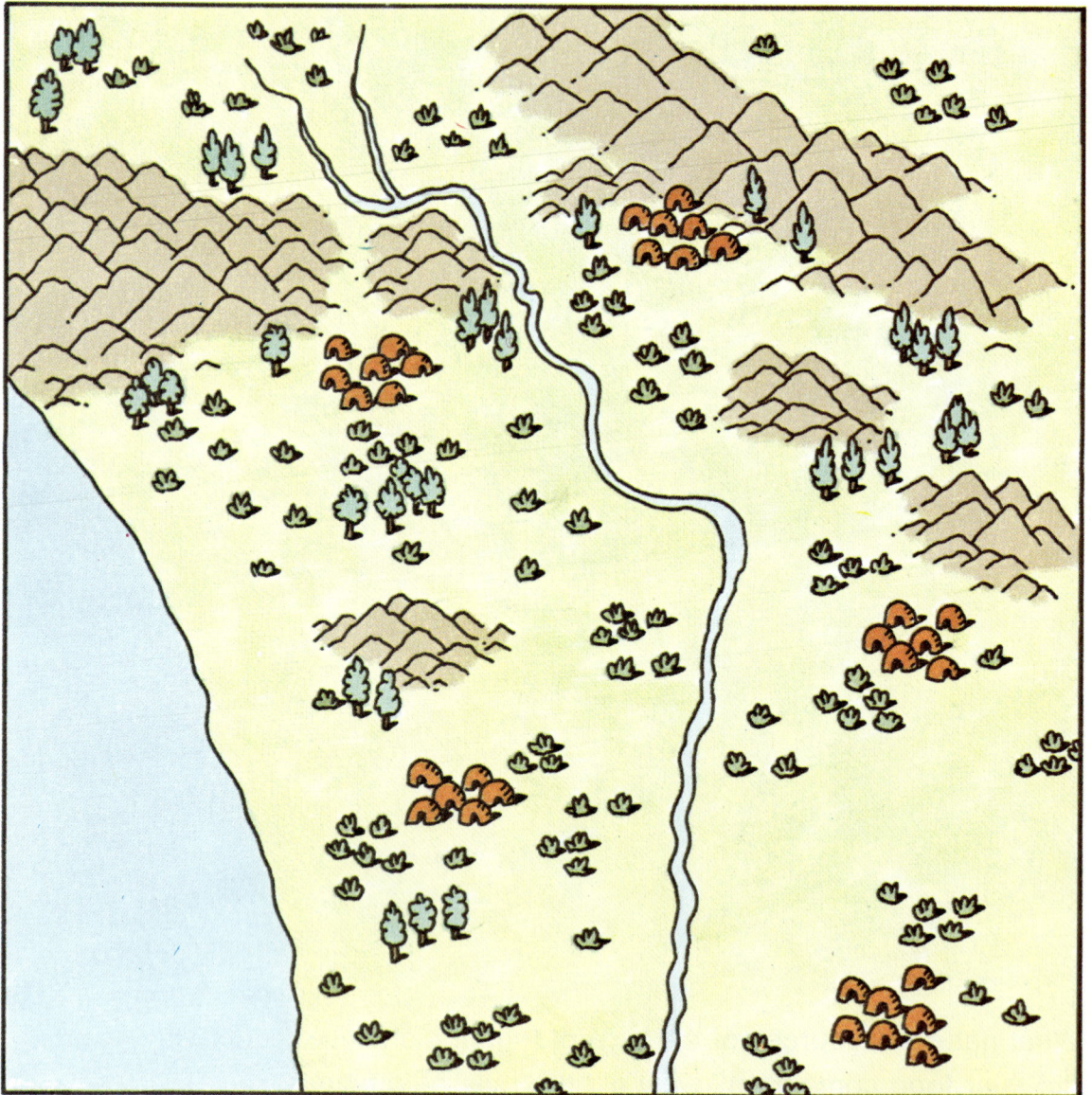

There was plenty of food. The Indians gathered fruits and nuts from the trees. They picked wild berries. The river provided them with fish.

One day people from Spain came looking for new places to live and work. They were **explorers**. The explorers liked this location. They knew it would be a good place for people to live. The explorers told people in Mexico about the place.

Why do you think the Spanish explorers liked this location?

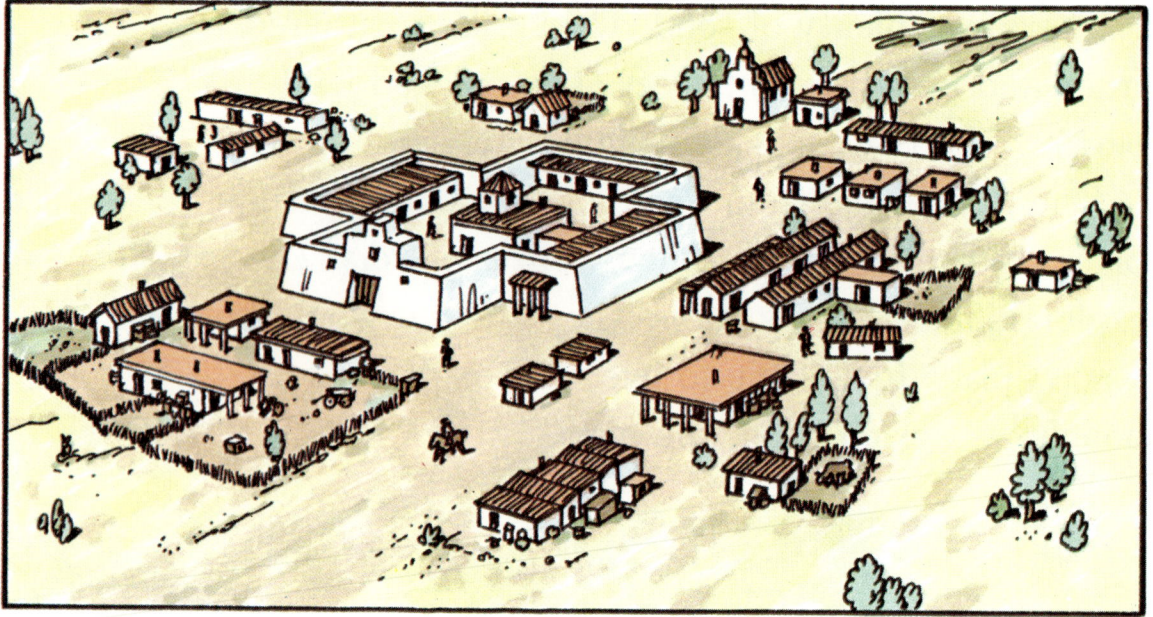

In time, people from Mexico came to the area to live. Some built churches called **missions**. Soldiers built a fort to protect the new people. Later, more people came and started a town. They named the town El Pueblo de Nuestra Señora, la Reina de Los Ángeles. In English this means "The Town of Our Lady, the Queen of the Angels."

Checking Up

1. Why did settlers begin the town of Los Angeles in this location?
2. What answer would you give to the key question at the beginning of this chapter?
3. *As years pass, what things do you think will help make this place change?*

Los Angeles Grows

As You Read

1. Think about these words.
   ranch   oil   industry
2. Look for answers to this key question.
   Why did Los Angeles grow?
3. Use this reading skill.
   You have learned many new social studies words. As you read on in this book, you will notice that these social studies words are used again and again. Go back to earlier chapters and test yourself to see if you remember the meanings of these words. If you cannot remember the meaning of a word, read the paragraph in which it appears in **bold**. The paragraph will help make the meaning clear to you. By testing yourself on the meanings of the social studies words, you will be able to understand these words when they are used in chapters to come.

The soldiers and people in the missions near Los Angeles needed farms to produce their food. More people came to farm the land. The population of the town of Los Angeles grew.

The soil was rich, and the weather was good for farming. Farmers grew fruits, vegetables, and grains. Other people started **ranches**. A ranch is a large farm where cattle, sheep, or horses are raised. The farmers and ranchers used water from the river for their crops and animals. Soon they produced more food than they needed. They began to trade their extra food for things they did not produce.

Transportation Helps the City Grow

More and more people moved to Los Angeles. Some came from Mexico. Others came from places in the United States. As time passed, railroads were built through the mountains. The railroads brought many new people to Los Angeles. The railroads were also used by farmers and ranchers to take their extra food to other parts of the United States.

Long ago many people moved to California in covered wagons. They traveled west across the Rocky Mountains.

Later many more people moved west by railroad. Trains such as this one helped Los Angeles grow in population.

Industry Helps the City Grow

Around 100 years ago, **oil** was found in Los Angeles. Oil is an important natural resource that comes from the ground. It is used for fuel and many other purposes. Many more people came to Los Angeles when they heard about the oil. Oil companies formed. People came to work in the oil fields.

Oil companies set up oil derricks to pump oil in Los Angeles.

Companies built airplane factories. People came to work in them.

Many early movies were made in Los Angeles. The warm, sunny weather allowed people to make movies outside year-round. Many movies are still made in Los Angeles today.

The population of Los Angeles grew and grew. Other **industries** besides the oil industry began to appear in the area. An industry is a type of work in which people produce and sell a special kind of product. These industries created many new jobs. More people moved to Los Angeles to work at these jobs. Other people came to work on nearby farms and ranches. Still others came to live in Los Angeles because of the good weather.

The People of Los Angeles

People came to Los Angeles from many places. Some came from other places in the United States. Some came from faraway places. Today there are many people in Los Angeles whose families came from China, Japan, or Mexico. Look at the Atlas map on pages 8–9. Find China, Japan, and Mexico. People came from other countries, too. Some people's families came to Los Angeles many years ago. Other families are newcomers to the United States.

141

The Way Movies Used to Be

The first movies ever made were different from the ones we see today. Early movies were silent. Instead of hearing what the actors said, the audience read what was said. Moviemakers had the spoken words printed and added to the movie. While the audience watched the movie and read what was being said, a person played the piano. It took many years for people to find a way to make "talking" movies, or movies with sound. Movies have come a long way since the days of silent movies.

Checking Up

1. How did farming, transportation, and industry help Los Angeles grow?
2. What answers would you give to the key question at the beginning of this chapter?
3. *What things have made your community grow or change?*

Los Angeles Today

As You Read

1. Think about this word.
   freeway

2. Look for answers to these key questions.
   a. How is Los Angeles today the same as early Los Angeles?
   b. What kinds of things make Los Angeles an interesting city?

3. Use this reading skill.
   Often two words mean the same or almost the same thing. We call these words synonyms. The social studies word *freeway* has a synonym. Find the sentence in this chapter where the word *freeway* is used. Another word in the same sentence is a synonym for freeway. Find this synonym. What other words can you think of that are synonyms for each other?

Ever since Los Angeles began, it has grown. Today Los Angeles is one of the largest cities in the United States. It is still growing. People come to live in Los Angeles for the same reasons they came in the past.

Los Angeles is an interesting city. Many people come to Los Angeles for their vacations. They visit places where movies and television shows are made. They visit the place where settlers first began the town of Los Angeles. There are many other sights to see, too. There are many special kinds of shops and restaurants to try.

Disneyland is a special place near Los Angeles. It provides recreation for many people.

People enjoy seeing where television shows are made.

As the population of Los Angeles grows, the needs and wants of the city grow as well. Like all cities, Los Angeles needs homes and schools for its people. Highways, or **freeways**, are built to provide good transportation for the millions of cars, trucks, and buses. The number of fire fighters, police officers, and other city workers must grow as the city grows. The people of Los Angeles work together to provide these and many other important things for their city.

Checking Up

1. Name two reasons that people still move to Los Angeles.
2. What answers would you give to the key questions at the beginning of this chapter?
3. *Will Los Angeles change in the years to come? If so, how do you think it will change?*

Graphs Tell a Story of Population Growth

Since Los Angeles began, its population, or number of people, has grown. One way we can show this population growth is to make a bar graph. The bar graph on page 147 shows the population for the city of Los Angeles in the years 1860, 1890, 1920, 1950, and 1980. Notice that the bars on the graph continue to get higher as time passes. The bar graph makes it easy to see how the population has grown over time.

1. In 1860 the population of Los Angeles was less than 5,000. By 1890 the population had grown to more than 50,000. How much did the population grow from 1860 to 1890?

2. In 1980 the population had almost reached what number?

3. If the population of Los Angeles was less than 5,000 in 1860, how much did the population grow between 1860 and 1980?

4. Between which two years shown on the graph did the population grow by about 1,000,000 people?

5. In the year 2000 do you think the population of Los Angeles will be larger or smaller than the population in 1980? Why?

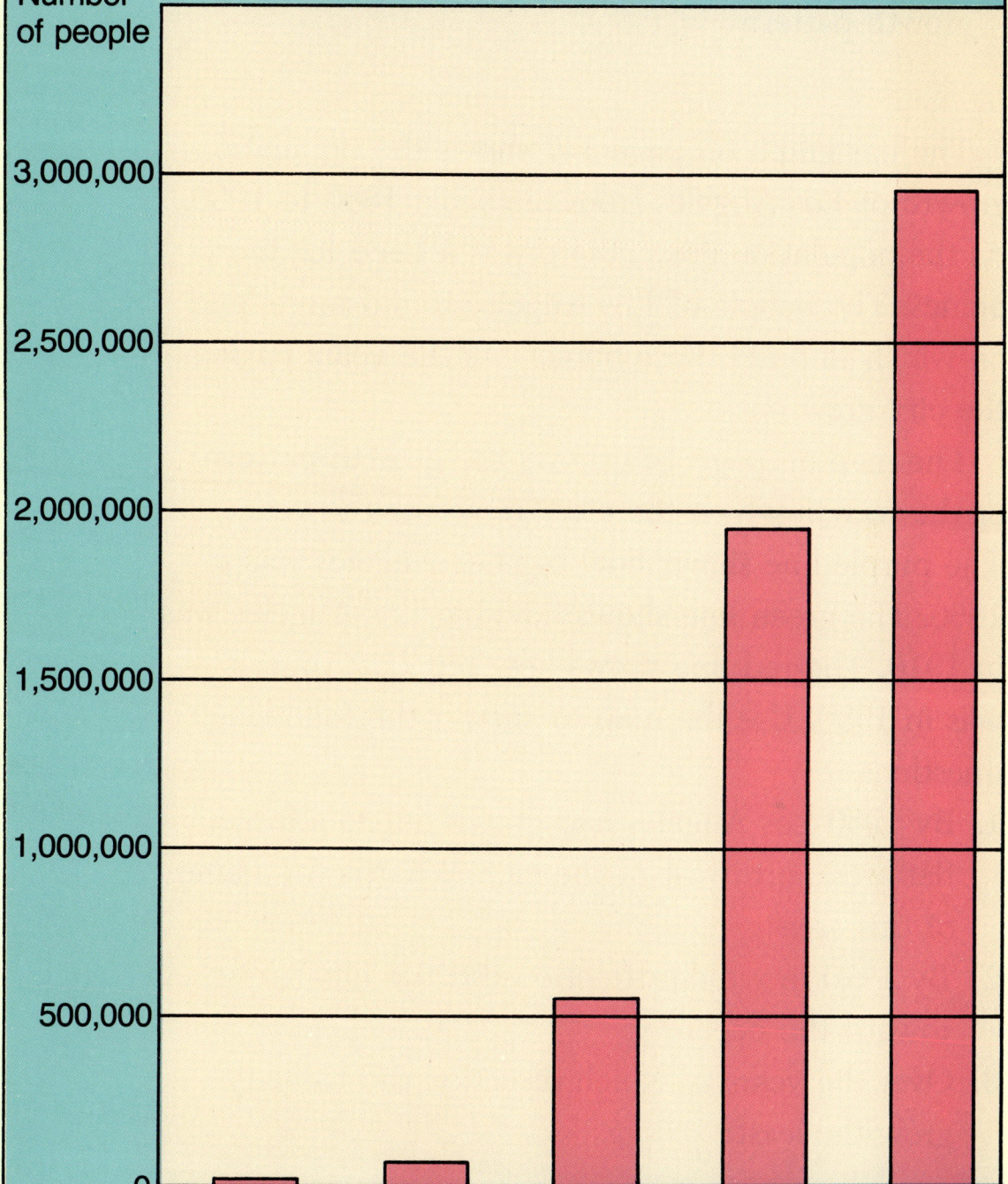

Population Growth of Los Angeles

Maps Tell a Story of City Growth

As you read, think about these words.
growth pattern

The bar graph on page 147 shows the population growth of Los Angeles from the years 1860 to 1980. As the population grew, there was a need for more homes. The people of Los Angeles found more land on which to build these homes. As the years passed, the city grew out.

The map on page 149 shows the **growth pattern**, or the way in which the city grew over the years. The purple line shows how big Los Angeles was in 1860. The green line shows how big Los Angeles was in 1910. The red line shows how big Los Angeles was in 1980. Use the map to answer the following questions.

1. By 1980 Los Angeles had grown out to a large, flat area northwest of the city. What is the name of this area?
2. By 1910 in which direction did the city grow toward the ocean?
3. Over the years in which direction did the city grow the least?

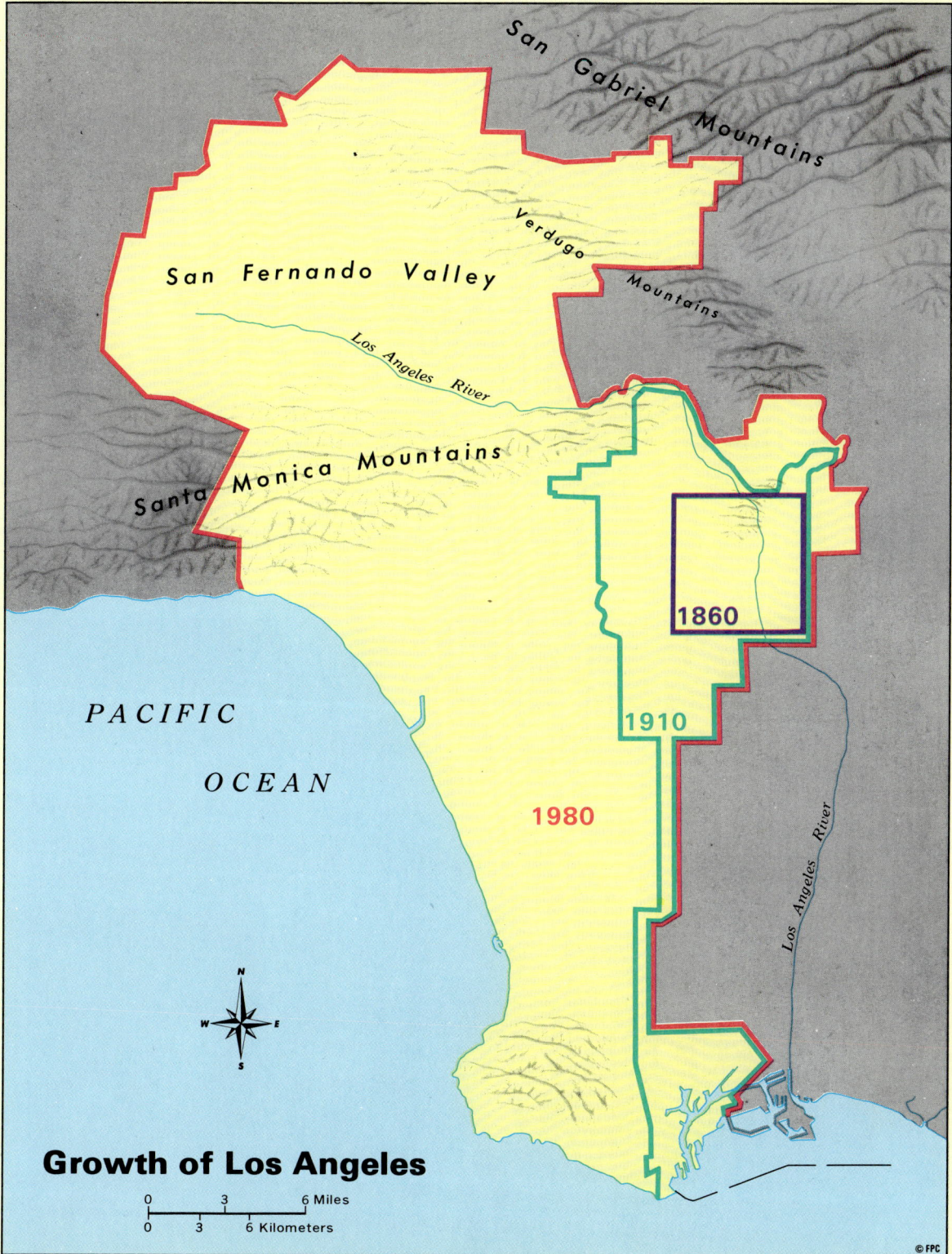

Growth of Los Angeles

San Gabriel Mountains

San Fernando Valley

Verdugo Mountains

Los Angeles River

Santa Monica Mountains

1860

1910

1980

PACIFIC OCEAN

Los Angeles River

N
W E
S

0   3   6 Miles
0   3   6 Kilometers

© FPC

Calcutta: Another City That Grew

As You Read

1. Think about this word.

   swamp

2. Look for answers to these key questions.

   a. Why did Calcutta grow?

   b. How are Calcutta and Los Angeles alike? How are they different?

Far away from Los Angeles is another city that grew. Look at the picture on page 150. This is a picture of Calcutta, a city in India. Calcutta is one of the largest cities in the world.

Find Calcutta on the map on pages 8–9. Calcutta is located on a plain close to the Hooghly River. Some of the land near the city is **swamp**. A swamp is soft, spongy land that is often covered by water. People do not live in the swamp. They live where the land is drier.

Hundreds of years ago, Calcutta was a small village. There were farms around the village. The weather in this location was good for farming. In the winter it was warm and dry. In the summer there were heavy rains. These rains helped the crops. People also used the water from the river for their crops during the dry winter.

The people in the village used the river for transportation, too. They took the crops they grew to trade with people in other villages.

One day new people traveled up the river. They came from Europe. They wanted to buy salt, rice, ginger, sugar, and tea. These were goods produced by people in the village. These villagers traded their goods for things they did not produce.

More people came to trade. Some of them stayed
in the village. Calcutta grew. It became a very
important trading center.

The people in Calcutta built new houses. They
built a hospital and a church. There were parks and
other places for recreation.

Many years passed. More and more people continued to come to Calcutta to live. Some came from Europe. Some came from other places in India. They came to get jobs. Today people still come to Calcutta looking for work. Some people get jobs working in factories. They manufacture goods that are used all around the world. Today millions of people live and work in Calcutta.

Workers in this factory make motors for cars. Other products made in Calcutta include rope, paints, and clothing.

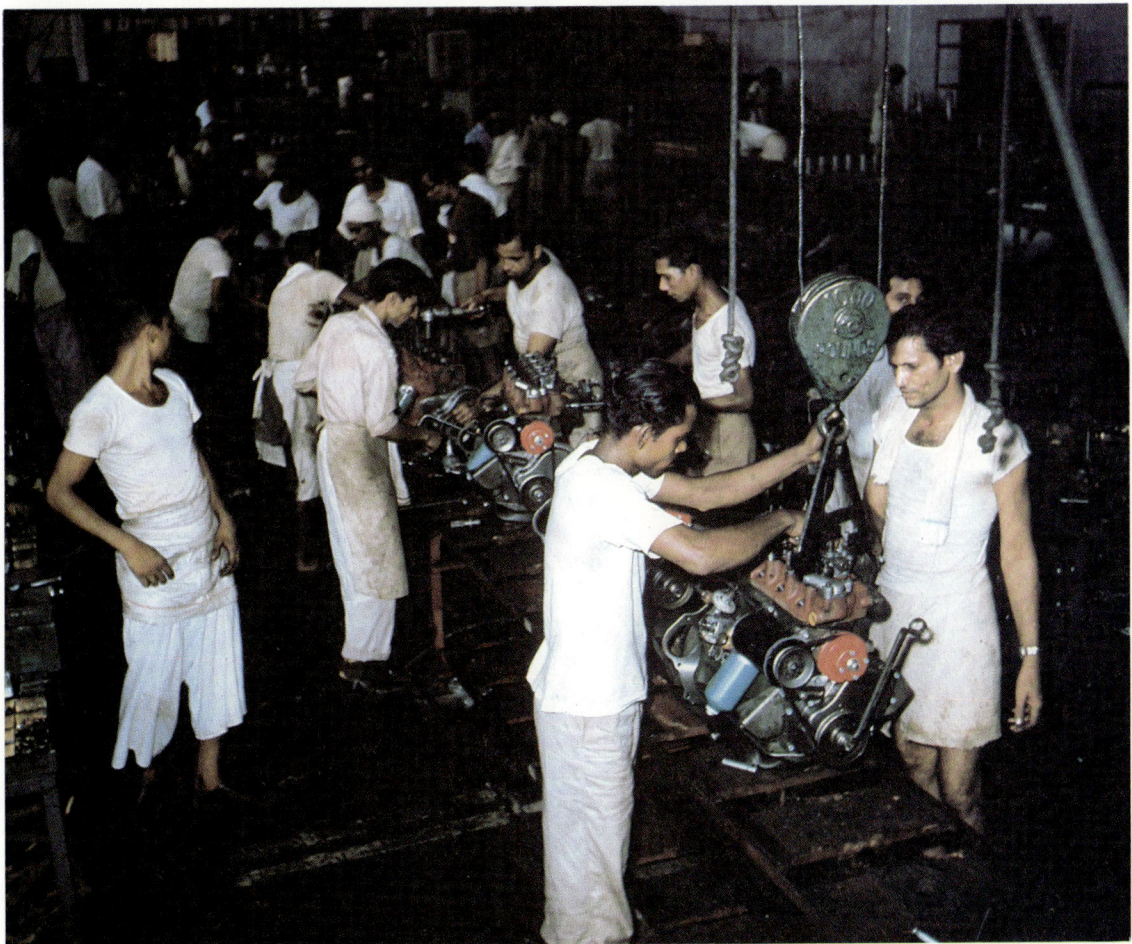

Big City Problems: Calcutta and Los Angeles

Both Calcutta and Los Angeles have grown very fast. People still move to these cities. Like all big cities, Calcutta and Los Angeles have problems. People in both cities work to solve these problems.

Everywhere you look in Calcutta, there are people. Some cannot find jobs or places to live.

Heavy traffic fills roads in and around Los Angeles and makes travel slow.

Mother Teresa

Some people in Calcutta are poor and have little food and nowhere to live. Mother Teresa is a Catholic nun who lives in Calcutta. She works hard to help many people with their problems. In 1979 she won the Nobel Peace Prize for her kind work helping others.

Checking Up

1. How did trade help Calcutta grow?

2. What answers would you give to the key questions at the beginning of this chapter?

3. *How can people solve Calcutta's problems?*

Unit 5 Summary

- Los Angeles and Calcutta are both large, growing cities.

- Farming, transportation, and industry helped Los Angeles grow.

- Trade helped Calcutta grow. Calcutta is still an important center of trade.

- Like all large cities, Los Angeles and Calcutta have problems that their people work hard to solve.

Unit 5 Review Workshop

What Have You Learned?

1. Who were the first people to live in the place where Los Angeles is located?
2. Name at least three reasons for the growth of Los Angeles's population.
3. Name one reason for the growth of Calcutta's population.
4. How are Los Angeles and Calcutta alike? How are they different?

Use Your Reading Skills

Decide if each sentence below describes Los Angeles or Calcutta. Find the one sentence that describes both cities.

1. People still come to this city to live and work.
2. People from Europe came to trade goods in this city.
3. This city is in India.
4. This city is located between mountains and the ocean.
5. People from Mexico began a town that grew to be this city.
6. Some of the land near this city is a swamp.
7. This city is in the United States.

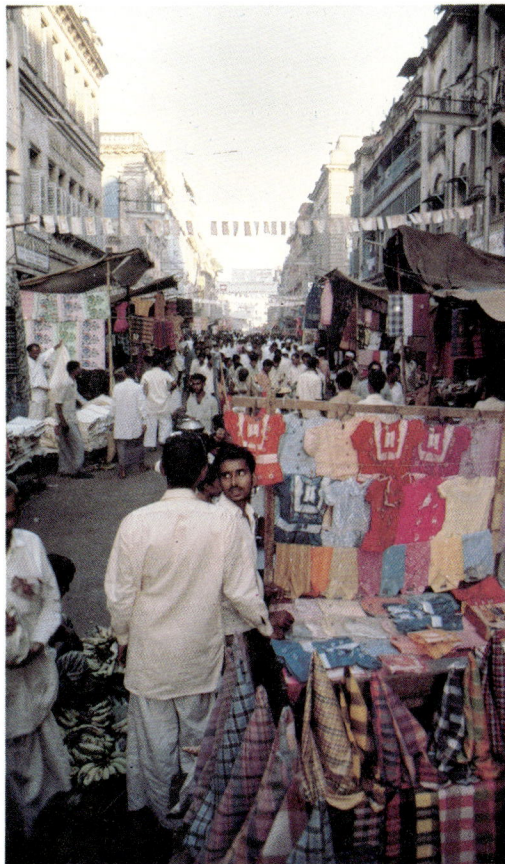

Use Your Writing Skills

The pictures above show three things you have studied in this unit. Use what you have learned to write a caption for each picture.

Learn by Doing

Pretend you are visiting either Los Angeles or Calcutta. Write a letter to a friend, telling what it is like to visit this city. Include information about people and places.

Unit 6

Cities Change

Philadelphia, Pennsylvania, has changed in many ways. Here tall new buildings climb high above the city's 200-year-old homes.

Growing Cities Need Space

As You Read

1. Think about these words.

   downtown   skyscraper

   suburb   apartment

2. Look for answers to this key question.

   How do cities find the space they need to grow?

Cities Grow Out

You have learned how Los Angeles and Calcutta grew. They grew because people wanted to live and work there. Because of growing populations, the cities needed space to build more homes. They needed space to build more factories and offices. Both cities grew by using more land. They grew out. The map on page 149 shows how Los Angeles used more and more land as the population grew.

Transportation makes it possible for cities to grow out. Roads connect the outside edges of a city to its **downtown**, or central business area, where many people work. People use cars, trains, and buses to work or shop in downtown areas. If people did not have these kinds of transportation, they would have to live close to their jobs. Cities could not grow out.

160

Often, as cities grow out, **suburbs** appear. Suburbs are smaller communities that develop near larger cities. Most suburbs are made up of many homes. Suburbs often have stores and shopping centers. Many people who live in suburbs work in nearby cities. They depend on the cities for many things. People can live in suburbs and work in nearby cities because of transportation.

Transportation made it easy for many suburbs like this one to begin.

Cities Grow Up

Many growing cities find the space they need by growing up. They grow up by building **skyscrapers**. Skyscrapers are tall buildings that have many floors. Some skyscrapers are more than 100 floors high. They use elevators to take people to each floor. Skyscrapers are used for offices, stores, and **apartments**. An apartment is a group of connecting rooms in which people live. Many apartments, offices, and stores can be in just one skyscraper. Although skyscrapers use only a small area of land, they have room for many people. By building skyscrapers, cities can use the space above them.

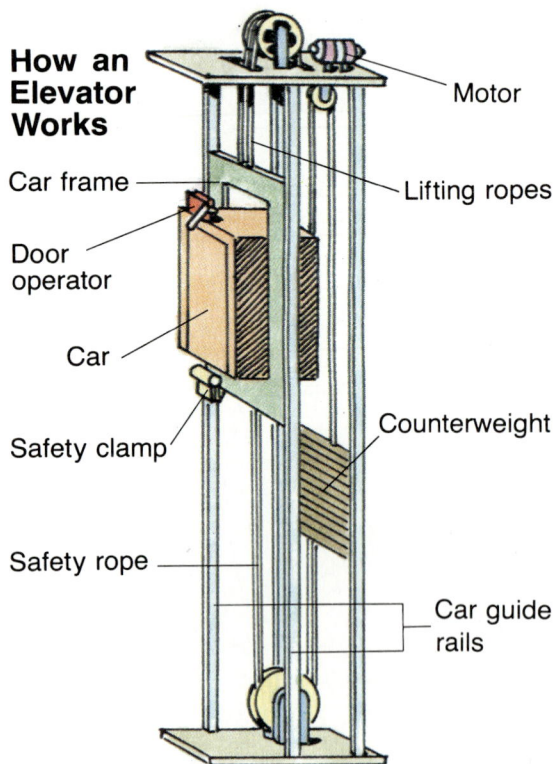

How an Elevator Works

Motor

Car frame

Lifting ropes

Door operator

Car

Counterweight

Safety clamp

Safety rope

Car guide rails

A person pushes a button on the wall outside the elevator. The hoisting ropes lower or raise the elevator car to the floor where the person is located. The doors open. The person enters the elevator and pushes the button for the floor where he or she wants to go. The doors close. Once again the hoisting ropes move the elevator car to the correct floor. The elevator stops, the doors open, and the person gets out.

Elisha G. Otis

Elevators were not always as safe as they are today. Many years ago the ropes that held up elevators sometimes broke. Then the elevators would fall, hurting the people inside them. A man named Elisha G. Otis had an idea. Over 100 years ago, he invented the first elevator that had a safety clamp. If the elevator ropes broke, the safety clamp kept the elevator from falling. After Otis's invention, people began building taller buildings. Elisha G. Otis helped make it possible for cities to grow up.

Checking Up

1. Name two different ways in which cities grow.
2. How does transportation help cities grow out?
3. What answers would you give to the key question at the beginning of this chapter?
4. *How have elevators helped cities grow?*

Houston Grows Up and Out

As You Read

1. Think about these words.
   high-rise   escalator
2. Look for answers to this key question.
   What does Carol Sue learn about Houston?
3. Use this reading skill.
   In this unit you will learn about three cities that have changed. They are Houston, Mexico City, and Philadelphia. As you read about these cities and look at the pictures in this unit, decide how these cities are alike. Also decide how these cities are different from one another.

Look at the picture of Houston on page 165. Houston is another large city in the United States. Look at the map on pages 12–13. In what state is Houston? What body of water is southeast of Houston?

Like Los Angeles and Calcutta, Houston's population has grown very fast. Houston is still growing today. It is growing in two different ways. It is growing up and out.

Carol Sue Visits Houston

Carol Sue Miller lives in a suburb of Houston. Her family has lived in the Houston area for many years. Carol Sue is proud to live near a city like Houston.

Carol Sue's mother is a teacher at one of the schools in their suburb. Carol Sue's father works for one of the oil companies in the city. Mr. Miller travels each day from their home in the suburbs to downtown Houston.

Houston, Texas, is a large, fast-growing city with buildings of many different sizes.

"Mom?" Carol Sue called one day as she came down the stairs for breakfast. "Next week is spring vacation for both of us. I was thinking. Can we do something special?"

"What would you like to do?" asked Mrs. Miller.

"I have an idea," answered Mr. Miller. "Why don't you two drive into Houston one day next week?"

"That's a good idea," Mrs. Miller replied. "We can visit Grandma. Carol Sue hasn't seen her new apartment."

"And we can all meet for lunch," added Mr. Miller.

"That sounds like fun!" exclaimed Carol Sue.

The following Wednesday morning, Carol Sue and her mother started their trip into Houston.

"Keep your eyes open, Carol Sue," said Mrs. Miller. "We haven't driven into Houston this way before." They had not gone very far when they drove past the Lyndon B. Johnson Space Center, named for former President Johnson.

"There's the space center. Our class went there on a field trip," said Carol Sue. "We learned a lot about rockets and space travel."

Inside the Johnson Space Center, scientists watch to see if the spaceflights go smoothly.

"Yes, Carol Sue," said Mrs. Miller, "the Johnson Space Center is a very interesting and important place. The rockets take off from Cape Canaveral, Florida. But after they are in the air, the people working at the space center are the ones who make sure everything goes well."

Carol Sue and Mrs. Miller drove on. The farther they drove, the taller and closer together the buildings were.

"Are we almost to Grandma's building?" asked Carol Sue.

"We're getting closer, but we still have a few miles to go," said Mrs. Miller. "Houston is a big city."

People enjoy watching sports teams all year under the plastic dome of the Houston Astrodome.

After some time Mrs. Miller and Carol Sue drove past a large round building. Its roof was shaped like a bubble. "There's the Astrodome," Mrs. Miller said. "It was the first sports field ever built with a roof. Teams can play baseball or football no matter what the weather is like."

"But how can they hit home runs if there's a roof over the baseball field?"

Mrs. Miller smiled. "The roof is very high. I don't know if anyone has ever hit a ball that high. Maybe someday we'll go to the Astrodome to see a baseball game. Then you'll see what it's really like." They drove on past Hermann Park. From the car, Carol Sue could see the large rose gardens.

"I remember this place," said Carol Sue. "Don't they have a zoo here, too?"

"Yes. A few years ago, we went with Grandma to see the animals," Mrs. Miller replied.

They reached the building where Carol Sue's grandmother lives. She has an apartment in a **high-rise**, or skyscraper, a few miles from downtown. Carol Sue and Mrs. Miller walked through the front door and called Grandma on the phone to tell her they had arrived. Then they went to the elevator.

"Press the button for the twelfth floor, Carol Sue," Mrs. Miller said. The elevator doors closed. When they reached the twelfth floor, the elevator doors opened. Carol Sue's grandmother was there to greet them.

Carol Sue went straight to the balcony. Looking down, she could see the Astrodome, Hermann Park, and many other places she recognized.

"What a view!" exclaimed Carol Sue. "I can see so much from up here."

"Yes, it's nice to be able to look out on the city," her grandmother replied.

While Mrs. Miller and Grandma visited, Carol Sue stood on the balcony, looking down at the city. "I wish I lived in a high-rise," Carol Sue said.

"Maybe you will someday," answered Mrs. Miller.

New skyscrapers fill the downtown area of Houston.

After some time Carol Sue, Grandma, and Mrs. Miller got in the car and drove toward the downtown area of Houston. When they reached downtown, Mrs. Miller parked the car. They walked down the street toward the Tenneco Building, where Mr. Miller works.

"Boy, Mom," Carol Sue said, "I feel so small next to all of these tall buildings."

"Yes, Carol Sue. Today Houston has many skyscrapers and other high-rise buildings. Just think how many people live and work in these buildings. Skyscrapers have helped Houston grow." Mrs. Miller went on. "When I was your age, Houston looked very different. It was much smaller, and it had fewer people. There were no tall buildings, and there were very few suburbs. There were just open fields on the land where our suburb is today."

"It's hard to think what it was like back then," Carol Sue said. "Everywhere you look today, there are people and buildings."

Grandma agreed. "Houston has changed a lot. It has grown faster than most cities in our country. It will probably keep on growing, too."

Carol Sue smiled. "I wonder what Houston will be like when I grow up."

They reached the Tenneco Building and got on the elevator. Mrs. Miller pushed the button for the twentieth floor, and soon they were standing in Mr. Miller's office.

"Let's eat underground," Carol Sue suggested. Everyone agreed. As they left for lunch, Carol Sue asked her father, "Dad, why is there an area underground?"

Mr. Miller explained. "Several years ago some people decided to use the space underneath the downtown area. They built stores and restaurants down there. A lot of people who work downtown go to the underground shops and restaurants on their lunch hours. By building the underground area, people made more space without using more land."

They walked a few blocks and then entered another building. They stepped onto the **escalator**, or moving stairs. It led to the underground. The lights from the stores and restaurants made everything bright and cheerful. Carol Sue spotted her favorite restaurant.

Today many cities like Houston are building restaurants and stores underground.

On the way home, Carol Sue kept thinking about the many ways Houston had found room to grow. It had grown up and out. It had even grown down.

After lunch it was time for Carol Sue and her mother to leave the big, tall city and return to their suburb.

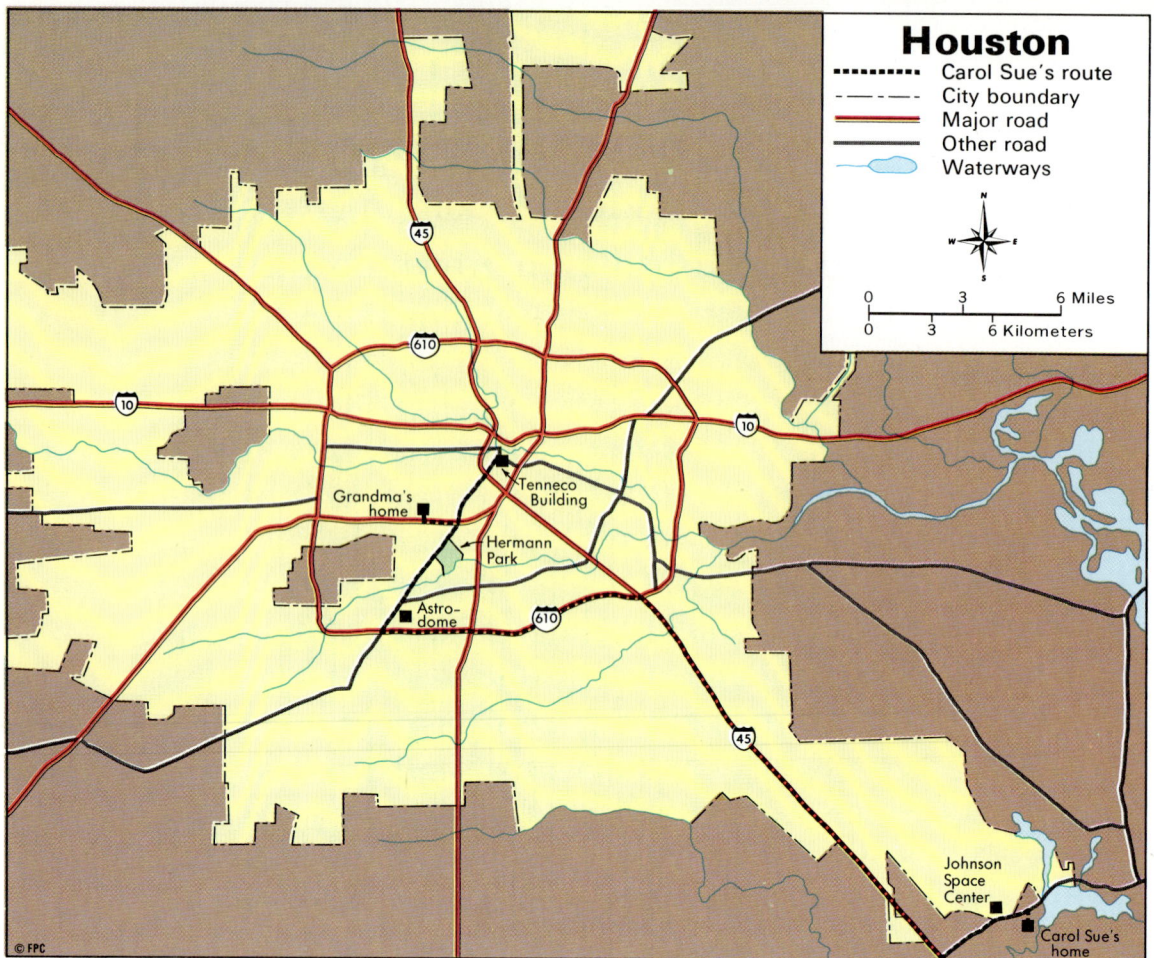

With your finger, trace Carol Sue's route into Houston.

Checking Up

1. How did Houston grow up and out?
2. How did Houston grow down?
3. How was Houston different when Mrs. Miller was Carol Sue's age?
4. What answers would you give to the key question at the beginning of this chapter?
5. *What do you think Houston will be like when Carol Sue grows up?*

Maps Tell a Story of Transportation

As you read, think about these words.

road map   interstate highway

Many people use maps to help them get from one place to another. Some of these maps are **road maps**. Road maps can show all kinds of roads. Some show city streets and some show big highways. Such maps help people get from place to place.

Look at the map on page 178. It shows some of the **interstate highways** in our country. Interstate highways are wide roads that connect two or more states. Notice that each highway has a number. Interstate highways that go east and west have even numbers. Interstate highways that go north and south have odd numbers. Use this map to help you answer these questions.

1. Does Interstate 80 go east and west or north and south?

2. Does Interstate 5 go east and west or north and south?

3. What interstate highway goes south through New York City, travels past Philadelphia, and goes through Washington, D.C.? What interstate highway goes through both Los Angeles and Houston?

4. Find your state on the map. What are the
   numbers of the interstate highways that go
   through your state? In which direction does each
   of these highways go? Put your finger on one of
   these interstate highways. Trace the way you
   would go to get to Philadelphia.

5. Put your finger on Chicago. Move your finger
   down Interstate 57 until you connect with
   Interstate 64. Go east on Interstate 64 until
   you connect with Interstate 75. Go south on
   Interstate 75. What city do you reach?

Interstate Highways

178

Mexico City Grows Up and Out

As You Read

1. Think about these words.

   history   island

2. Look for answers to these key questions.

   a. How are Mexico City and Houston alike? How are they different?

   b. Who were the first people in the area to find more space for their growing city?

Carlos Ramirez lives in Mexico City. It is the largest city in North America. Find Carlos's city on the map on pages 8–9. In what country is Mexico City? In which direction is this country from the United States? Like Houston, Mexico City is a city that has grown up and out.

One day Carlos's teacher, Mr. Vega, asked the class, "How many of you can tell me something about our city?"

"It's very big," said one boy. "It's very old, too."

"Yes," replied Mr. Vega. "The city was started many, many years ago by the Aztec Indians. Today I am going to tell you the story of our city. We call this kind of story the **history** of our city. I will show you pictures that will help tell the story." The class listened and watched as Mr. Vega began.

"The Aztec Indians built their city on an **island**. An island is a piece of land with water on all sides of it. This island was in the middle of a lake.

"The city grew. Soon the Indians needed more space. They had an idea. The Indians made large rafts and covered them with mud. Then they planted trees and crops on the rafts.

"The roots of the trees grew down into the water. As time passed, the roots grew right into the bottom of the lake! These floating islands became as strong as the real island. The Aztecs made new land where once there was only water. They solved the problem of finding space for their growing city.

"Many years passed. Explorers from Spain came to the city. They built a Spanish city in the same place as the Aztec city. After more time the Spanish people who settled here drained some of the water from the lake. Then they had even more land.

"The city continued to grow and change for many, many years. Mexico City needed even more space! Like many other cities around the world, Mexico City found new space by growing up. Skyscrapers were built.

"Several years ago a strange thing began to happen. Some of these skyscrapers began to sink as much as a foot every year. They were sinking because the land under our city was once the bottom of a lake. The land is very spongy and still full of water. Now there is something very special about the skyscrapers built in our city. Today's skyscrapers have special supports built under them. These supports, or platforms, keep the skyscrapers from sinking.

Mexico City is a beautiful city with both old and new buildings. Some buildings, like this one, have pictures painted on them.

"Well, class," said Mr. Vega, "I have told you how Mexico City found space by growing up into the sky. You also know that Mexico City has grown out. More and more land has been used by the city. Like many other cities, Mexico City has many suburbs around it. People move to the suburbs because there is more land. People who move to the suburbs often work in the city.

"Our city has changed in many ways over the years," said Mr. Vega. "As more people move here, it will change even more. When your children are grown, our city may still have more people than any other city in the world."

Later, as Carlos walked home from school, he thought about what Mr. Vega had taught the class. That night Carlos told his family what he had learned about their city.

"Yes, Carlos," said his mother. "Our city has a long and interesting history. It is one of the oldest cities in North America."

Checking Up

1. How did the Aztecs make more room for their growing city?
2. What is special about the skyscrapers built in Mexico City?
3. What answers would you give to the key questions at the beginning of this chapter?
4. *Why do you think Mr. Vega believes that Mexico City will go on being the largest city in the world?*

Cities Get Old: Philadelphia

As You Read

1. Think about these words.
   settler   shipping center
2. Look for answers to these key questions.
   a. Why is Philadelphia an important city?
   b. Why did Philadelphia change?

We have learned that many cities change by growing larger. Cities change in other ways, too. Some cities change by growing old. This is the story of Philadelphia, an important city that grew old.

Philadelphia Begins

Hundreds of years ago **settlers**, or people moving to a new land, came to the area that was to become Philadelphia. They liked the location. It was near a river that flowed toward the Atlantic Ocean. The land was good for farming. They knew this location would be good for a town. Around 1682 the settlers named their town Philadelphia. The name means "brotherly love." Find Philadelphia on the map on pages 12–13.

The settlers wanted their town to be a place where people could live as free people. They wanted Philadelphia to be a place where people could practice what they believed was right. Many people came to live in Philadelphia for these reasons.

As time passed, people also came to Philadelphia to work. Because the nearby river led into the Atlantic Ocean, Philadelphia became an important **shipping center**. Ships carried manufactured goods in and out of the city. Shipping and manufacturing companies provided jobs for many newcomers. Philadelphia grew and grew. More and more homes were built. Soon Philadelphia was a city.

By 1702 Philadelphia was an exciting, growing city where many industries were located.

The Birthplace of Our Nation

Before our land became the United States, Philadelphia and other early settlements were ruled by the king of England. Many settlers did not want to be ruled. They believed that every person should be free and equal. They wanted to start their own country and write their own laws.

Around 1774 important leaders began to hold meetings in Philadelphia to decide what to do. After many talks these leaders decided to tell the king of England how they felt. In 1776 they wrote the Declaration of Independence. It told the king that the people wanted to have their own free country. The settlers fought a war in order to be free.

A few years later leaders met in Philadelphia again to write the Constitution of the United States. This paper was for the people of our nation. It told how the people planned to run the new country. We still follow this plan.

The Declaration of Independence and the Constitution of the United States are important parts of our nation's history. Because these two papers were written in Philadelphia, we sometimes call Philadelphia "the birthplace of our nation." From 1790 to 1800, Philadelphia was the capital of the United States.

Benjamin Franklin

Benjamin Franklin was a famous citizen who lived in Philadelphia around the time our country first began. He started the city's first fire department. He found ways to speed up the mail service and helped raise money for a city hospital. Franklin began a program to pave, clean, and light the streets of his city. As an important American leader, he helped write the Declaration of Independence. He was also an inventor. The people of this nation will always remember Benjamin Franklin.

Philadelphia Keeps Growing

As the years passed, many industries began in Philadelphia. Many people came to the area to work as coal miners. Other big industries began to produce ships, trains, machines, iron, textiles, and clothing. The city had become an important place. It continued to grow.

Some of Philadelphia's older buildings became run-down and needed repairs.

Philadelphia Changes

Philadelphia grew for many years. Then slowly other cities started new industries and became important. People began moving to the other cities to look for jobs. Few new people moved to Philadelphia. Over the years the population of Philadelphia became smaller. People did not build as many new homes and other buildings. The city was growing old.

Checking Up

1. Why is Philadelphia called "the birthplace of our nation"?
2. After many years, why did Philadelphia's population stop growing?
3. What answers would you give to the key questions at the beginning of this chapter?
4. *What do you think the people of Philadelphia might have done to help their city?*

Philadelphia Gets Restored

As You Read

1. Think about this word.
   restore

2. Look for answers to these key questions.
   a. Why did the people of Philadelphia feel proud of their city?
   b. How did the people of Philadelphia help their city?

3. Use this reading skill.
   At the back of the book, you will find a list of subjects—people, places, and things—talked about in this book. This list is called the Index. An index helps you locate information in a book. Turn to the Index. Notice that the subjects are listed in the order of the alphabet. Find the listing for Philadelphia. The numbers that follow are the pages on which you will find information about Philadelphia. To what pages can you turn to find this information? Think of another subject you have studied in this book. Use the Index to help you locate the pages that tell about that subject.

Philadelphia had grown old, but many people were still proud of their city. Philadelphia was the birthplace of our country. Important Americans like Benjamin Franklin had lived there. Although some of the city's homes and other buildings were now old and needed repairs, people at one time had taken care of them.

People did not want these interesting old homes and buildings to be torn down. They decided that they would work hard to **restore** these places. To restore buildings means to make them look like they did when they were first built. Let's take a look at one house that was built long ago.

It takes many workers to restore a building to the way it looked when it was first built.

Samuel's Home

Samuel Thompson lived in Philadelphia many, many years ago. This is the street where he lived. The brick homes on the street were called town houses. Each home shared a wall with the home next to it. The streets were paved with round stones called cobblestones.

Samuel's house had a fireplace in every room. The fireplace kept the rooms heated in winter. The kitchen fireplace was used for cooking.

Lisa's Home

Lisa Bailey lives in Philadelphia today. She lives in the same town house that Samuel Thompson lived in almost 200 years ago. Like the other houses on the street, Lisa's house has been restored.

The people who restored Lisa's house wanted to make it look the way it did many, many years ago. Cracks in the walls were fixed. A new roof and new stairs were built. They replaced some boards in the floor and painted the house. Some things were added to Lisa's house to make it more modern. Electricity, running water, and heaters were put into the town house.

By restoring buildings to their old style, homes like Lisa's remain very special. Lisa is proud of her old home, which looks very much today as it did when it was first built.

Important Places Get Restored

Because the people of Philadelphia care about their city, many famous places have been restored. Today you do not have to look at pictures to see how Philadelphia looked when the Declaration of Independence and the Constitution were written. You can walk through restored neighborhoods and see for yourself.

People believe that Betsy Ross sewed the first United States flag in this house.

The Liberty Bell and Independence Hall are important parts of our country's early history.

People in Savannah, Georgia (left), and Louisville, Kentucky (right), are restoring parts of their cities, too.

Checking Up

1. Why did the people of Philadelphia want to restore parts of their city?
2. What answers would you give to the key questions at the beginning of this chapter?
3. *Besides restoring buildings, how else can people take care of their communities?*

Unit 6 Summary

- Cities find the space they need by growing up and out.
- Suburbs are smaller communities that develop near larger cities.
- Both Houston and Mexico City are cities that grew up and out.
- Philadelphia is an old, important city that has been restored in many areas.

Unit 6 Review Workshop

What Have You Learned?

1. How do skyscrapers, or high rises, help cities grow?
2. What are suburbs?
3. Why is transportation important to growing cities?
4. Name at least three things that Houston and Mexico City have in common.
5. Why is Philadelphia important to our country's history?
6. What did the people of Philadelphia do to restore parts of their city?

Use Your Reading Skills

Think of facts you learned about Philadelphia while reading this unit. Study the picture of Philadelphia on page 196. How many facts about the city can you name from looking at the picture? What are they?

Use Your Map Skills

Look at a road map of your state. Locate your community. If your community is not shown on the map, locate a community nearby. Use the map key to help you find the symbol used for interstate highways. Which interstate highway runs the closest to your community? In which direction does this interstate highway go? What interstate would you take to get to your state capital? In which direction would you be traveling on this interstate to get to the state capital? What is the total number of interstates that pass through your state?

Learn by Doing

Talk to some adults who grew up in your community. Ask them how the community has changed since they were your age. Draw a picture that shows what you think your community looked like then.

Unit 7

Cities Can
Be Planned

On the Fourth of July, fireworks add to the beauty
of our country's capital, Washington, D.C.

Washington, D.C.: The Planned City

As You Read

1. Think about this word.

   engineer

2. Look for answers to these key questions.
   a. Why did people of long ago start the city of Washington, D.C.?
   b. Why is Washington, D.C., an important city?

Each of us has made plans. Maybe your family has taken a trip. Before you leave, you plan where you will go. Sometimes you make plans with a friend to do something special. Many things we do every day are planned.

Sometimes groups of people make plans, too. They may plan a new building or a new park. They may even plan how a city will look! People can make important decisions about their city. Sometimes they can decide where their city will be located and in which direction it will grow. They can decide where streets will go and how many houses will be built.

Look at the picture on page 201. This is Washington, D.C., the capital of our country.

It is a beautiful city. There are statues, parks, and great buildings. Washington, D.C., is the home of the President of the United States. Many lawmakers of our country work in this city. It is one of the most important cities in the world. It is a planned city.

Planning Our Capital

Many years ago there was no city where Washington, D.C., is today. Before people from Europe settled in America, there was an Indian village in the area. Later, the settlers from Europe started a small trading town nearby called George or George Town.

In the early years of our country, several different cities were the capital of our nation at one time or another. They included New York, Baltimore, and Philadelphia. Many leaders of our country did not want the capital to be in any of these cities. They did not want their new capital to be in any one state. They wanted a special place for the city.

It was hard to decide where the capital would be. It took six years to find a place. Finally, the states of Virginia and Maryland gave land for the new capital city. George Washington, the first President of the United States, picked out the exact spot. He picked a place along the Potomac River. Many people thought the river would be useful as a transportation route. The city was named after George Washington.

George Washington had grown up in the area around the Potomac River. He knew it would be a good place for the capital.

By choosing Pierre L'Enfant (right) to plan Washington, D.C., George Washington (left) made sure that the United States would have a good capital city.

Once the location was found, the city could be built. How does a new city begin? The leaders of the country wanted a beautiful city. They wanted a city that would have space in which to grow. George Washington knew that this new city had to be planned carefully.

President Washington hired a French **engineer**, Pierre L'Enfant, to plan the new city. An engineer decides how and where roads, bridges, and buildings should be built. Pierre L'Enfant was happy to be chosen. He loved this new country. He wanted to plan a beautiful city with wide streets and grand buildings.

There are many questions that have to be answered when a new city is planned: Where will the streets be? Where will the houses be built? Where will stores and companies be located? For Washington, D.C., there was another important question: Where would the buildings be in which leaders of our nation could meet and make important decisions?

L'Enfant finally decided the answers to these questions. He drew a plan for the city. It showed in a simple way what the city would look like. Look at the picture on this page. It is the plan L'Enfant had for the new capital of the United States. Notice the squares and circles where some of the streets come together.

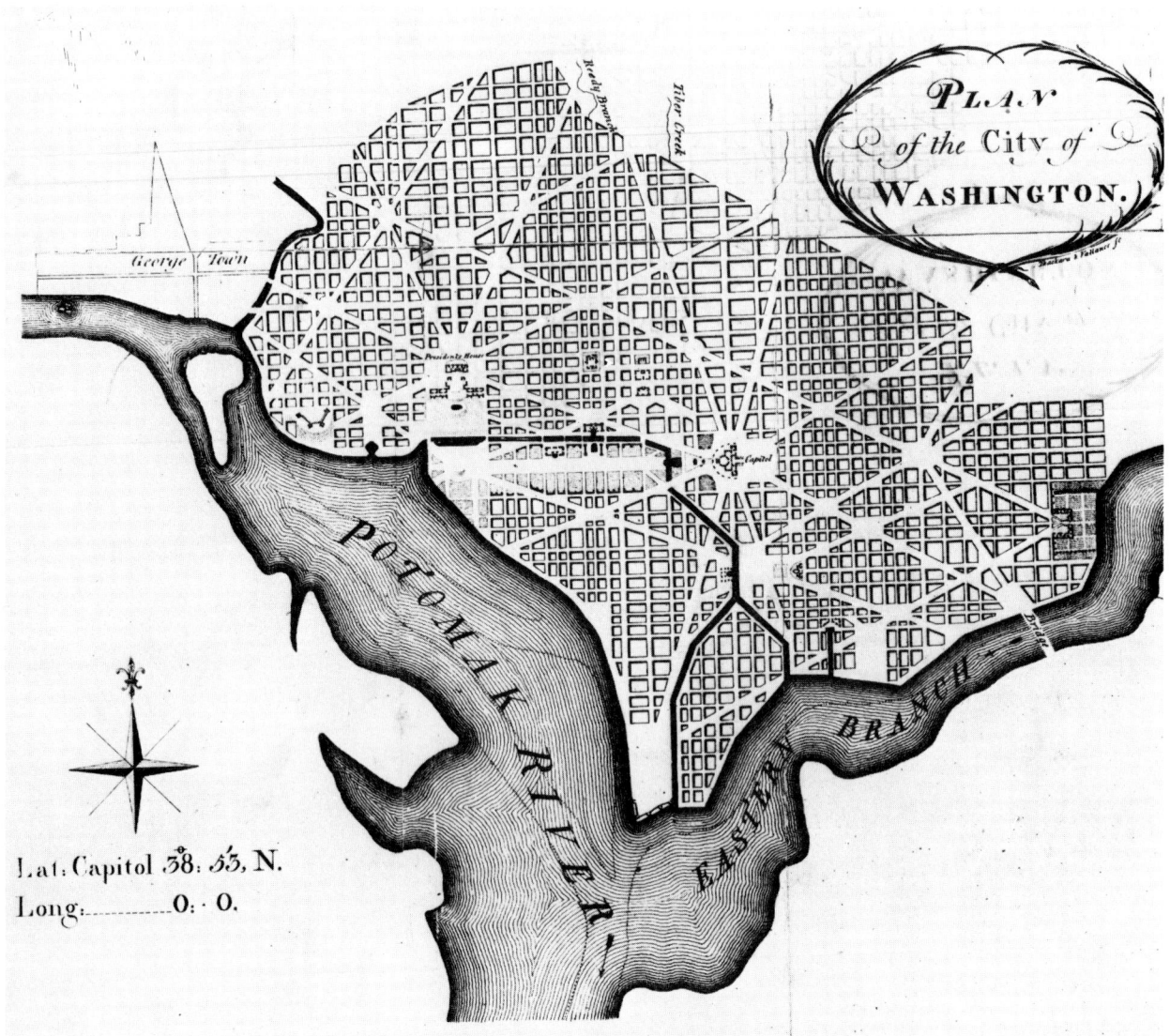

Benjamin Banneker

Planning a city like Washington, D.C., took a lot of work. Someone had to measure the land and decide where the city borders were going to be. This kind of work was done by surveyors. Benjamin Banneker was one surveyor. He and a man named Andrew Ellicott helped Pierre L'Enfant plan Washington, D.C. Using a special tool to measure land, Banneker helped figure out just how much land there was for the new capital. Banneker did many other important things, too. He wrote a book about the stars and about weather. He invented a special kind of clock. He also fought for the right of all people to be free.

Once the capital was moved to its new location, Washington, D.C., grew fast.

The United States did not have a lot of money for its new capital city. Work on the new city went very slowly. Finally, in 1800, the capital was moved from Philadelphia to Washington, D.C.

Checking Up

1. Who picked the location for our new capital? For whom is our capital named?
2. What answers would you give to the key questions at the beginning of this chapter?
3. *How did planning help Washington, D.C., become a beautiful city?*

Washington, D.C., Today

As You Read

1. Think about these words.
   memorial   monument   Capitol
2. Look for answers to this key question.
   Why do people like to visit Washington, D.C.?
3. Use this reading skill.
   Sometimes when you read, you come to a word you have never seen before. When this happens, it is important to stop and find out what the word means. You might use a glossary or a dictionary. Sometimes the sentence itself helps you understand the new word. Besides learning what a new word means, it is important to find out how to say, or pronounce, the new word. The Glossary in this book helps you pronounce many new words. Turn to the Glossary and find the three new social studies words listed above. Notice that each word is divided into smaller parts, or syllables. Say each syllable slowly. Then put the sounds of the syllables together to make the new word. Using the Glossary, practice saying the other new social studies words in this unit.

Washington, D.C., has grown and changed since it first became the capital of our country. However, Pierre L'Enfant's basic plan for the city can still be seen. Look at the present-day picture below. Statues and buildings have been built in certain circles and squares. Some of these statues and buildings were built to help us remember famous Americans. They are called **memorials** or **monuments**. They are important to all Americans.

The White House is the home of the President of the United States.

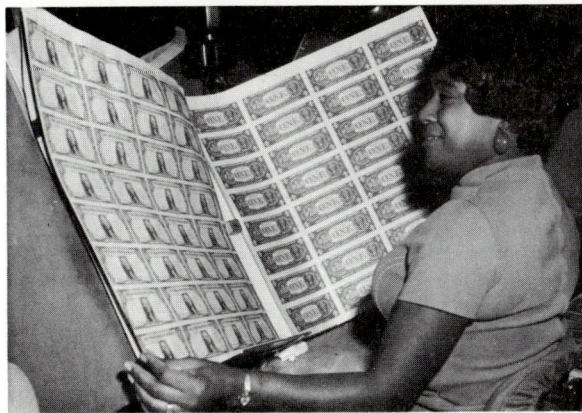

Visitors can see how money is printed at the Bureau of Engraving and Printing.

Many Americans visit Washington, D.C., every year. They want to see where the President of the United States lives. They want to see where our money is printed. Many people like to visit a building called the United States **Capitol** to see how laws are made. Notice that its spelling is almost the same as the word *capital*. There are many interesting places to visit in Washington, D.C.

These pictures show only some of the places to visit in Washington, D.C.

These three famous places were built to honor three Presidents of the United States.

The Washington Monument stands high above other places in the capital.

Inside the Lincoln Memorial, visitors can see a large statue of the sixteenth President.

This memorial helps us remember the third President of the United States, Thomas Jefferson.

Lawmakers from around the country meet in this room (above) in the Capitol Building. Many people visit the Capitol Building (left) each year.

Checking Up

1. Name three monuments or memorials in Washington, D.C.
2. Name the building where lawmakers meet to make important decisions.
3. What answers would you give to the key question at the beginning of this chapter?
4. *How do you think the early leaders of our nation would feel about their capital city if they could see it today?*

Maps Tell a Story of Location

As you read, think about this word.

grid

There are many interesting places to visit in Washington, D.C. Each year people from many parts of the country travel to Washington, D.C., for the first time. They use maps to help them find the places they want to visit.

Look at the map of Washington, D.C., on this page. Notice the blue lines on the map. These lines cross to form boxes. These lines and the boxes they form are called a **grid**. A grid makes it easy to locate places on a map.

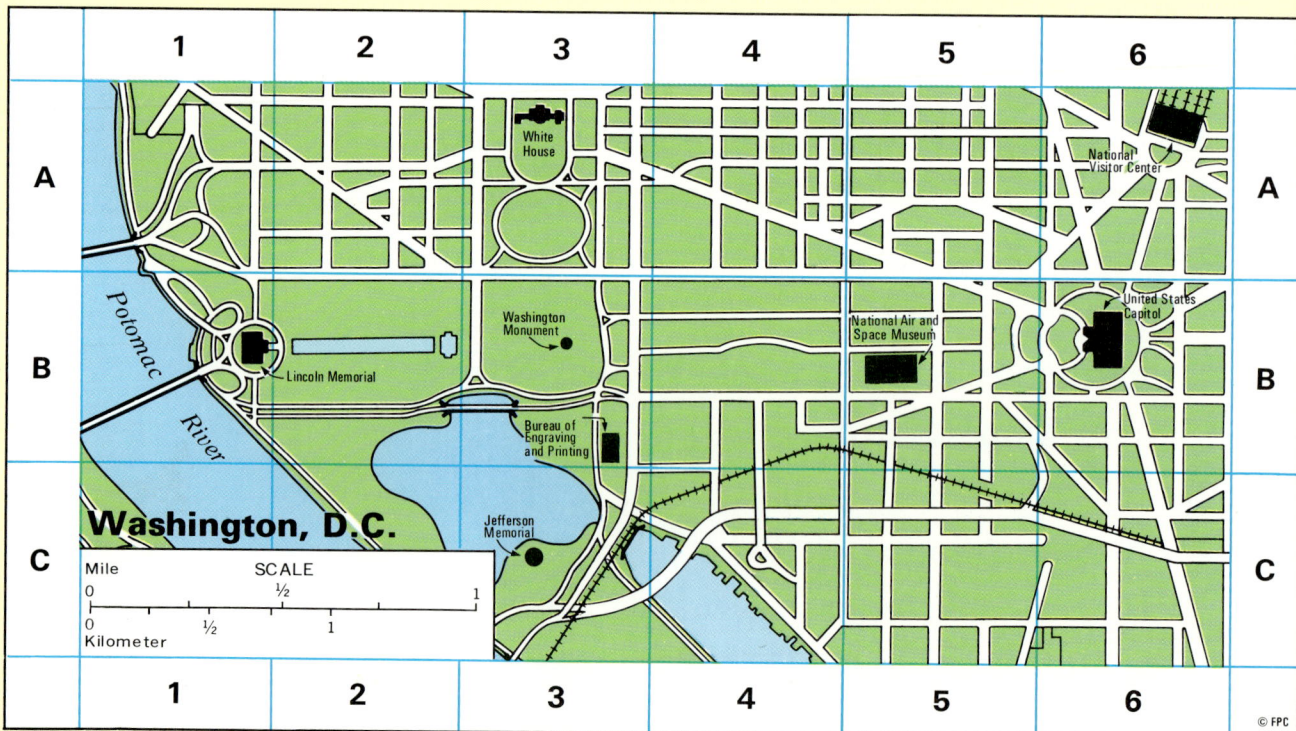

	1	2	3	4	5	6
A			White House			National Visitor Center
B	Potomac River / Lincoln Memorial		Washington Monument / Bureau of Engraving and Printing		National Air and Space Museum	United States Capitol
C	Washington, D.C.		Jefferson Memorial			

Washington, D.C.

Mile
SCALE
0   ½   1

0   ½   1
Kilometer

© FPC

Look at the numbers that go across the top and across the bottom of the map. Look at the letters that go down both sides of the map. Put your finger on the letter A. Move it across the map until it is under the number 3. This box is called A-3. The White House is located in A-3.

See if you can locate these other important places in Washington, D.C.

Name	Location
Lincoln Memorial	B-1
Washington Monument	B-3
Jefferson Memorial	C-3
Bureau of Engraving and Printing	B-3

A list of places and grid locations helps visitors find the places they want to visit. Grids can make maps easier to read.

1. What interesting place is located in B-5?
2. What important building is located in B-6?
3. What building is located in A-6?
4. Which row of grid boxes shows the largest number of places—row A, row B, or row C?
5. Which grid box is in the northeast corner of the map? Name the building located in that corner.
6. Find at least four grid boxes on the map that do not show any important buildings, monuments, or memorials. Name these boxes.

Another Planned City: Canberra

As You Read

1. Think about this word.
   hemisphere
2. Look for answers to these key questions.
   a. Why did people build Canberra?
   b. Why was it important to plan Canberra?
   c. Why is Canberra important to the people of Australia?
3. Use this reading skill.
   This chapter is about another city, Canberra, Australia. Canberra is far away from Washington, D.C. It is on the other side of the world. Still, there are many things that the two cities have in common. Both cities are planned. Both cities are important. The people of both cities speak the same language. As you read this chapter and study the pictures, look for other ways in which Canberra and Washington, D.C., are alike. Also, look for ways in which the two cities are different. Be ready to talk about what these likenesses and differences are.

The picture on this page shows another planned city. It is Canberra, Australia. Like Washington, D.C., Canberra is a capital city. It is the capital of the country of Australia. Australia is located in the southern half, or **hemisphere**, of the earth. It is south of the equator. Australia is also a continent. Find Australia on the map on pages 8–9. In what part of Australia is Canberra located?

Many years ago, around 1901, Australia became a new country. The people wanted a beautiful, new, planned city to be built as their nation's capital. In 1908 leaders of the country chose the location of the capital city, Canberra.

The location chosen for the new capital city was in the open country where very few people lived.

A contest was held to see who could draw the best plans for the new capital. People from around the world entered the contest. An American from Chicago, Illinois, won. His name was Walter Burley Griffin. Look at his plan on this page. Now look back to Pierre L'Enfant's plan for Washington, D.C., on page 204. How are the two plans alike? How are they different?

It took many years for Canberra to be built. People worked very hard to make their capital city look the way Walter Burley Griffin had planned. Finally, the capital city was completed.

It took many workers like these people to turn open land in Australia into the nation's capital city.

Through the years Canberra has grown. However, the city still looks very much the way Walter Burley Griffin planned it to look.

Like our Capitol Building, Parliament House is the place where lawmakers meet to make important decisions.

Walter Burley Griffin planned this beautiful lake in the middle of the city. Later, the lake was named after him.

Parks in Canberra are located away from noisy traffic. This was one of the many things planned for the city.

Canberra has a planned transportation system. There are special lanes on the streets that are for buses only.

Checking Up

1. How are Canberra and Washington, D.C., alike? How are they different?
2. What answers would you give to the key questions at the beginning of this chapter?
3. *Why is it important to plan new cities like Canberra?*

Unit 7 Summary

- Some cities are planned before they are built.
- When a city is planned, someone must decide where the city will be, how big it will be, and where streets, homes, and buildings will be located.
- Washington, D.C., is the capital of the United States of America.
- Canberra is the capital of Australia.
- Washington, D.C., and Canberra are both planned cities.
- Washington, D.C., and Canberra are both beautiful and important cities. They both have many places for people to visit.

221

Unit 7 Review Workshop

What Have You Learned?

1. Name at least three decisions that have to be made when a city is planned.
2. Why did people in the United States want a new city to be built for their capital?
3. Who chose the land for the United States capital?
4. Why is Washington, D.C., an important city?
5. How are Washington, D.C., and Canberra alike? How are they different?

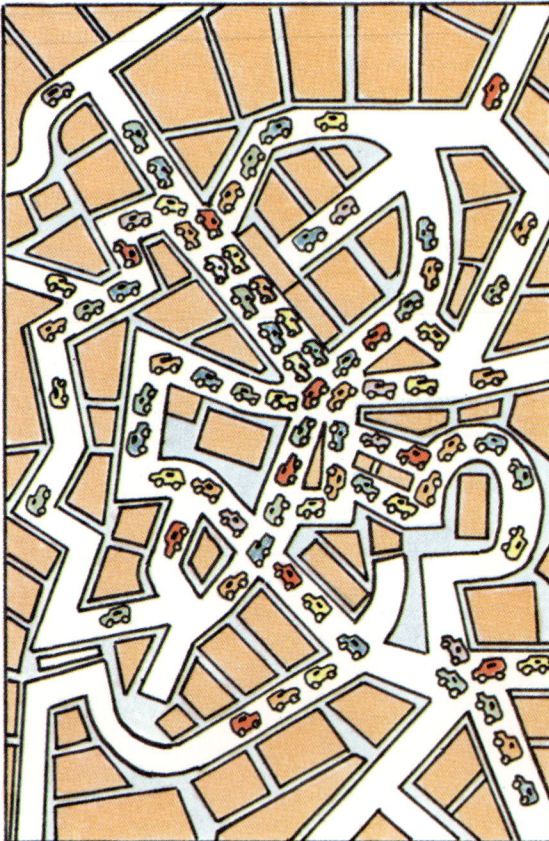

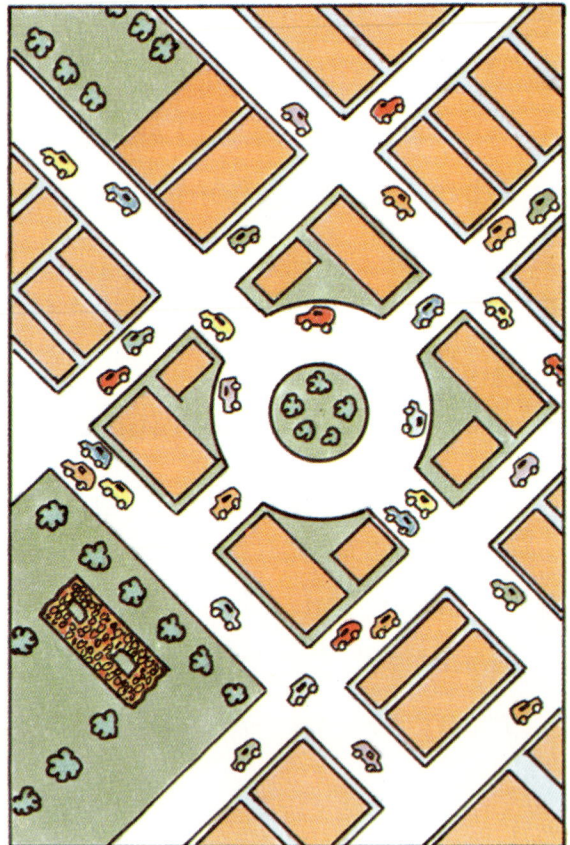

Use Your Reading Skills

Look at the two pictures of cities on page 222. Which city is planned? Which city is not planned? How can you tell?

Use Your Speaking and Listening Skills

In a group of three or four people, plan your own make-believe city. Decide on a location for your city. Will it be near a river or a lake? Will the land be flat, or will it have mountains? How big will your city be? Where will houses, apartments, and other buildings be located? Where will the streets and parks be located?

Share your plans with another group. Give reasons for your decisions. Listen to the other group's plans and the reasons it gives. How are the plans alike? How are they different?

Learn by Doing

Think about the ideas your group and the other group talked about in the exercise above. On your own, write down what you think were the best ideas discussed for planning a city. You may want to choose some ideas from your group and some from the other group. Draw a plan for a city that uses these ideas.

Unit 8

The Future

The Woodlands, Texas, is a community that has been planned for the future.

Everything Changes

As You Read

1. Think about this word.
   future
2. Look for answers to these key questions.
   a. How have you changed?
   b. What might some of the changes be in the world in the future?

Things change. They do not stay the same.
Cars change.

How we dress changes.

What we do for fun changes.

You change. You are growing up. How have you changed since you were a baby?

You have changed in many ways. You will continue to change as you get older. You will learn many new things. You will meet new people. Someday you will be grown up. You will choose to do things that are important to you. What do you think you will be doing when you grow up?

Just as people change, the world changes. When you are older, the world will be different from the world today. How will the world you live in change?

When we talk about what will happen in the years to come, we are talking about the **future**. In the future, the population of the world will be larger. You have learned that people need food and shelter. In the future, the need for food and shelter will be greater than ever. More food will be needed to feed all the people. People will need places to live. Towns and cities will grow. They will need more space than ever before.

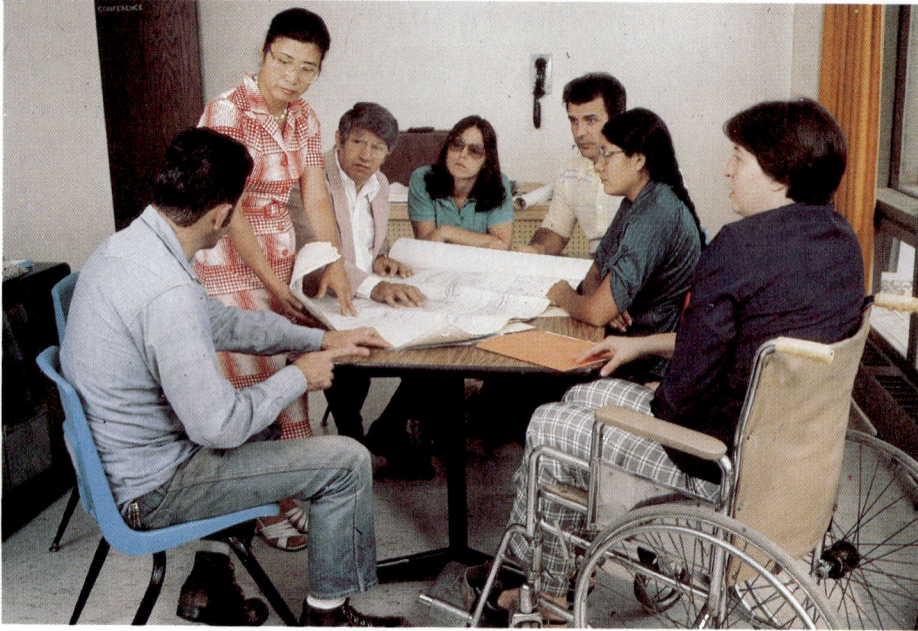

This group of people meets to discuss how they would like their community to look in years to come.

People are already planning for the future. Some are trying new ways to grow food. Some are making new plans for cities. Others are working with new sources of fuel. There have always been people with new ideas. These ideas are the keys to the future.

Checking Up

1. What things do we already know about the future?
2. What answers would you give to the key questions at the beginning of this chapter?
3. *In what ways do you think you will change in the years to come?*

Food for the Future

As You Read

1. Think about these words.

    desert   hydroponics

    greenhouse   sea farming

2. Look for answers to this key question.

    In what new ways are people producing food?

3. Use this reading skill.

    On page 229 you learned that the world
    population will be larger in the future than it is
    today. In the rest of this unit you will read about
    plans people are making to provide basic needs
    for the future population. The growing world
    population is causing people to make these plans
    for the future. As you read the rest of this unit,
    make a list of the plans that some people are
    already making.

Because the world population will be larger, we
will need more food to feed everyone. Some people
think we can use more land for farming. However,
most of the good farmland in the world is already
being used. Some people have already begun looking
for new ways to grow and raise food.

Crops in this desert greenhouse get a watering from one of the workers.

Greenhouses

Growing crops in the **desert** has always been hard to do. The air and land are very dry. Desert areas do not get the rain that crops need.

Some farmers irrigate their fields when there is not enough water. This allows them to grow crops in desert areas. A few scientists have also been able to grow crops in the desert inside large glass-covered or plastic-covered buildings called **greenhouses**. The soil, air temperature, lighting, and amount of water are controlled inside the greenhouses. Insects and weeds cannot get in. These conditions are perfect for growing crops. By using greenhouses, these farmers of the future can grow many different kinds of crops. Greenhouses can be used in the desert, on frozen land, and in many other places where crops usually cannot grow. The more crops that can be grown, the more food there will be to feed the people of the future.

Hydroponics

Because there will be more people in the world in the future, we will need more land on which to build towns and cities. Some land that could be used for farming might have to be used for apartments or houses. However, there is a way to grow food without using any land at all. It is called **hydroponics**.

Hydroponics means "water gardening." Plants are grown in water instead of soil. Plants grown in water do not produce as many roots as plants in soil. These plants do not need to have as much space between them. More plants can be grown in water than in the ground. Hydroponic farming is already being used to grow some vegetables. In the future, many food crops might be grown this way.

Careers

A Plant Scientist

A person who works with plants is called a plant scientist. Plant scientists go to school to learn about growing crops. They learn what plant food the crops need in order to be healthy. Some plant scientists look for new ways to grow crops. They want to find the best ways to produce food for the future.

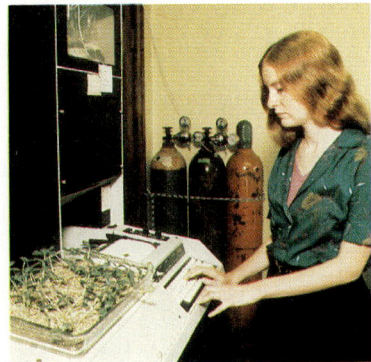

Birds sit and rest on the dividers of this sea farm. Below, fish swim in their special areas.

Sea Farming

In the future, more of our food will come from the oceans. Fish will be raised in much the same way as farmers raise animals today. This kind of farming is **sea farming**. Large numbers of fish are raised in certain areas of the ocean. These areas are closed off from the rest of the ocean. Then the fish will not swim away. Workers make sure that all the fish in the sea farms have enough food. Some people think that most of our fish will someday come from these farms.

Checking Up

1. What is a greenhouse? What does *hydroponics* mean? What is sea farming?
2. What answers would you give to the key question at the beginning of this chapter?
3. *Why do you think some people have already begun looking for new ways to produce food for the future?*

Cities of the Future

As You Read

1. Think about this word.
   pedestrian
2. Look for answers to this key question.
   Where will people live in the future?

Where will you live when you are older? In the future, people will still live on farms and in towns. However, many more people will live in cities.

Earlier in this book, you learned that cities provide goods, transportation, recreation, and many other things for people. Because more people will live in cities in the future, the need for these important goods and services will be even greater than it is today. City leaders will have to work to make sure their cities are good places to live.

Today some people are beginning to think about where and how people will live in the future. They have started building brand new cities for the future. Like Washington, D.C., and Canberra, these cities are planned. However, these new cities are even more planned than Washington, D.C., and Canberra. The people who have planned the new cities have decided how large the city populations will be. They have even planned the homes for the people. They want their cities to be places where workers can find jobs. The new cities will also provide recreation and transportation. The planners want their new cities to be clean, safe, and beautiful. Let's take a look at some new planned cities that have already begun.

Cumbernauld

Cumbernauld is a new community in the country of Scotland. One interesting plan for Cumbernauld has been its system of paths for **pedestrians**, or people who walk. These paths are far away from streets so pedestrians will be safe. Planners built Cumbernauld to have a population of about 70,000. When the population reaches 70,000, no more people will be allowed to live there.

The Woodlands

The Woodlands is a new community in Texas. It is twenty-eight miles north of Houston. It was started in 1974. It will not be finished until the year 2000.

The Woodlands is being built in the middle of a forest. Planners want to leave as much of the natural beauty of the forest as possible. They have carefully

Cumbernauld, Scotland, is a new community that has
many different kinds of homes and other buildings.

planned how many homes and other buildings will
be built and where they will be located. Planners
have decided that the Woodlands, like Cumbernauld,
will have a limited population.

Other new cities have been started in different
places around the world. These cities have been
planned for the future. As the world's population
grows, more of these planned cities will be started.
Maybe, when you are grown, you will live in a
planned new city.

Checking Up

1. Name at least three decisions often made by
   planners of brand new cities.
2. What answers would you give to the key question
   at the beginning of this chapter?
3. *If you planned a new city for the future, what
   kinds of things would you include? Why?*

Maps Tell a Story of Land Use

As you read, think about these words.

land-use map   residential   employment

Columbia, Maryland, is located near Washington, D.C. It is another new city built for the future. Planners of Columbia gave a lot of thought to the best way to set up their community. Once the city boundaries were made, the planners had to decide how they were going to make use of the land. The map on page 239 is called a **land-use map**. It shows how the planners of Columbia chose to use the land in their community.

Look at the map key. Areas where homes are located are called **residential** areas. Areas where people work are called **employment** areas. Using the map key, locate the residential and employment areas in Columbia. Is more land used for residential areas or for employment areas? Use the land-use map to answer more questions about Columbia, Maryland.

1. What is the symbol used for recreation areas? How many recreation areas does Columbia have?
2. Locate the downtown area of Columbia. Why do you think many roads lead to the downtown area?
3. What other land-use symbols are used on this map?

Land Use
Columbia, Maryland

SCALE
One inch equals 1 mile

Key
≡	Interstate road
—	Road
■ (red)	Shopping mall
■ (yellow)	Downtown
■ (pink)	Residential area
■ (brown)	Employment area
■ (green)	Open space
● (teal)	Recreation area
~ (blue)	Lake

4. Find the recreation area that is the farthest east.
   Use the map scale to find out how many miles
   this recreation area is from the downtown
   shopping mall.

Future Cities in Unusual Places

As You Read

1. Think about these words.
   floating city   space city

2. Look for answers to this key question.
   Where else besides on land might people live in the future?

3. Use this reading skill.
   On pages 4–5 at the beginning of this book, there is a list of all unit titles you have read during the year. This list is called the Table of Contents. When starting a book, a table of contents can tell you about what you are going to read. It can also tell you what page to turn to in order to find information about a certain subject. Now that you have reached the end of this book, you can use the Table of Contents for another purpose. Turn back to pages 4–5. Read the unit titles and chapter titles to review what you have studied in this book. When you come to a title that you do not remember as well as you would like, look up the page number on which it begins. Skim through the pages of the unit.

Someday people may live on floating cities like this one.

In the future, people may live in places where they have never lived before. Some people are already making plans for these new, unusual cities.

Floating Cities

In the future, more land will be used for homes and for growing food. Some cities will completely run out of land. Some scientists have already thought of new ways to build cities without even using land. One way is to build cities on water. These cities would be built on gigantic platforms that would float on the ocean. **Floating cities** would be very much like cities on land. They would have apartment buildings, parks, airports, and all the other things cities on land have.

What do you think it would be like to live in a space city like this model shows?

Space Cities

There is another way that people might solve the problem of not having enough land. Cities of the future may be built in space. Large space stations may someday hold entire communities. These **space cities** would make their own fresh air and water. Then people could live far, far away from the earth.

You and the Future

What do you think the future will be like? Where do you think you will live in the future? Much of what happens in the future depends on the plans and choices people make. As you grow up, you will also help make plans and choices for the future. What kind of future would you like to help plan?

What will the world be like?

I wonder what it will be like when I am a grown-up.

What will I be?

How would I like the world to be?

Checking Up

1. Why have people begun to make plans for floating cities and space cities?

2. What answers would you give to the key question at the beginning of this chapter?

3. *If you were to begin planning for the future today, what would be your first plan?*

Unit 8 Summary

- As years pass, both people and the world change.
- In the future, the world's population will be larger than it is today.
- Some people are finding new ways to produce more food.
- Others are planning communities for the future.
- Much of what happens in the future depends on the plans people make for it.
- As you grow up, you will also help plan the future.

Unit 8 Review Workshop

What Have You Learned?

1. In the future, why will the need for food and shelter be greater than ever?
2. In what ways have people begun to plan for the future?
3. Why is planning for the future so important?

Use Your Reading Skills

Read the sentences below. Decide which sentence best describes the future.

1. We must wait and see what the future will be like.
2. What happens in the future depends on the plans and choices people make.
3. The future will be the same as the present.
4. We will have many problems in the future.

Use Your Time Skills

A time line is a kind of graph. It shows when things happened. You read time lines from left to right. Look at the time line on page 245. Katie made it to show what happened last summer.

What was the first event Katie listed on her time line? What was the last event? Did Katie go fishing before or after her birthday? What happened

June 11	June 29	July 17	Aug. 4	Aug. 22	Sept. 9

June 11
School
ended.

July 1
My
birthday!

July 19
I went to
visit Grandma.

Aug. 25
I got new
shoes.

June 20
We went
fishing.

Aug. 8
I came home
from
Grandma's.

Sept. 5
School
started
again.

July 4
Parade

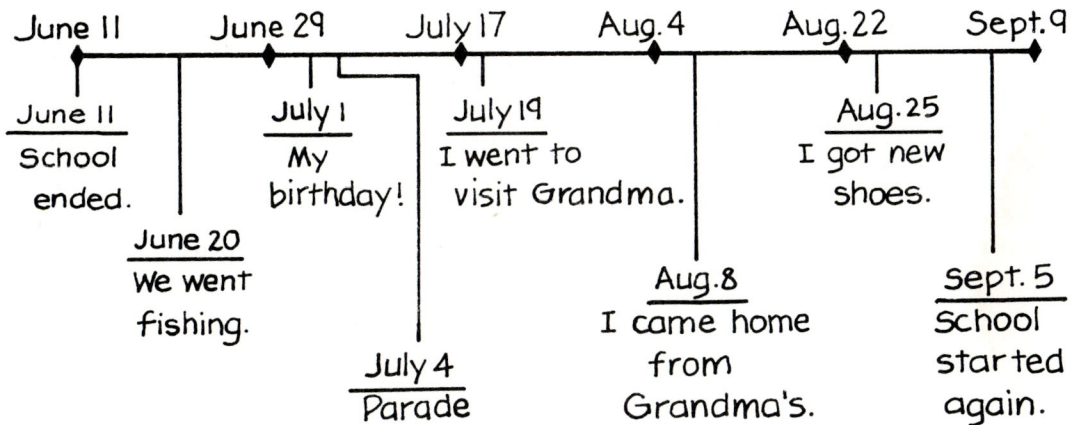

between Katie's birthday and her visit with her grandmother?

Time lines can show more time than just the length of a summer. You can make a time line that shows important things that have happened during your entire life. Start by making a line. On the left end of the line, mark off the year you were born. Then add a mark for each year of your life. The last mark on the right end should be for this year. Label each mark with the year it stands for. Think of an important event that happened in each year of your life. Write this event by the correct year.

Learn by Doing

Draw a picture that shows what you would like your home to look like when you are grown up.

Glossary

This is the Glossary. It tells you the meanings of many words found in this book. Notice that the Glossary words are in the order of the alphabet. This will help you find the meanings of words more easily. Also notice that each word is divided into parts, or syllables, and that heavy accent marks (′) and light accent marks (′) have been added to help you say each word correctly. Use the Glossary often. It will help you pronounce, spell, and understand the meanings of the words you read.

acre (a′cre) An area of land about the size of a football field.

ancient (an′cient) Very old.

apartment (a·part′ment) A group of connecting rooms in which people live. There are usually several apartments in a single building.

bar graph (bar graph) A chart with colored bars to show how much or how many.

border (bor′der) A line on a map that divides one area of land from another.

business (busi′ness) The buying and selling of goods and services.

capital (cap′i·tal) The city where a country's leaders meet to make laws.

Capitol (Cap′i·tol) A building in a capital city in which leaders of the country's government meet and make many laws.

career (ca·reer′) The job a person has to earn money.

citizenship (cit′i·zen·ship′) The rights and duties of being a member of a community and of a country.

city (cit′y) A large community where many people live. A city has more people than a town.

coast (coast) Land along an ocean.

communication (com·mu′ni·ca′tion) Any way people share news and ideas by reading, writing, listening, or speaking.

community (com·mu′ni·ty) A place where people live, work, and play near one another.

company (com′pa·ny) A group of people who work together.

compass (com′pass) A tool that is used to find direction on the earth.

compass rose (com′pass rose) A drawing that shows directions on a map.

Constitution (Con′sti·tu′tion) A paper written by early leaders of the United States. It tells the basic laws of our country.

continent (con′ti·nent) One of the seven largest bodies of land on the earth.

decision (de·ci′sion) A choice.

declaration (dec′la·ra′tion) A public statement.

depend (de·pend') To need.

desert (des'ert) A dry area of land where few plants can grow.

dictionary (dic'tio·nar'y) A book that lists most words of a certain language and their meanings.

distance (dis'tance) How far it is from one place to another.

downtown (down'town') A main business area of a city where many people work.

east (east) A direction. East is to the right of a person facing north.

electricity (e·lec'tric'i·ty) A kind of energy used to produce light, heat, and power.

elevator (el'e·va'tor) A machine that goes straight up and down, bringing people to each floor of a tall building.

employment (em·ploy'ment) Work at a job.

engineer (en'gi·neer') A person who decides and plans how and where roads, bridges, and buildings should be built.

equator (e·qua'tor) An imaginary line on the earth halfway between the North and South poles. The equator is found on many globes and maps.

escalator (es'ca·la'tor) A moving stairway that takes people up and down.

explorer (ex·plor'er) A person who visits new places to discover facts and to bring back information.

factory (fac'to·ry) One or more buildings where people and machines make new goods.

farm (farm) A place where crops are grown or animals are raised.

floating city (float'ing cit'y) A city of the future that would float on a platform in the ocean.

freeway (free'way) A highway.

fuel (fu'el) Anything that is burned to give heat or power. Oil, gas, coal, and wood can be used as fuel.

future (fu'ture) The years to come.

globe (globe) A model of the earth.

goods (goods) Things people grow, raise, or make.

greenhouse (green'house) A glass-covered or plastic-covered building in which plants are grown.

grid (grid) A set of lines that cross to form squares.

growth pattern (growth pat'tern) The way in which a city or town grows.

harvest (har'vest) To gather a crop from the fields when it is ripe.

hemisphere (hem'i·sphere') Half of a sphere.

high rise (high rise) A skyscraper.

hill (hill) A rounded part of the earth's surface with sloping sides, smaller than a mountain.

history (his'to·ry) The story of things that happened in the past.

hydroponics (hy'dro·pon'ics) A way of growing plants in water.

in-between direction (in'-be·tween' di·rec'tion) A direction halfway between two main directions.

independence (in'de·pen'dence) Freedom.

industry (in'dus·try) A type of work in which people produce and sell a kind of product.

interstate highway (in'ter·state' high'way) A wide road that connects two or more states.

inventor (in·ven'tor) A person who makes something that no one has ever made before.

irrigate (ir'ri·gate') To bring water to land for growing crops.

island (is'land) An area of land, smaller than a continent, with water on all sides of it.

key (key) A list of symbols used on a map.

landform (land'form') The shape of the land. Plains, mountains, hills, and plateaus are landforms.

land-use map (land'-use map) A map showing how people use land.

law (law) A rule.

lawmaker (law'mak'er) A person who helps make laws.

location (lo·ca'tion) The place where something is.

logger (log'ger) A person who works in the forest cutting down trees for wood.

logging community (log'ging com·mu'ni·ty) A community in which many people work in the forest cutting down trees for wood.

lumber (lum'ber) Wood used to build things.

manufacture (man'u·fac'ture) To make goods, often in large amounts.

manufacturing community (man'u·fac'tur·ing com·mu'ni·ty) A community in which many goods are produced.

map (map) A drawing showing where towns, cities, rivers, countries, and other things are located.

map scale (map scale) The size of a place shown on a map.

market community (mar'ket com·mu'ni·ty) A community in which people buy and sell goods.

mayor (may'or) The elected leader of a city or town.

memorial (me·mo'ri·al) A statue or building built to help us remember famous people; a monument.

mission (mis'sion) A settlement where church people live and work.

monument (mon'u·ment) A statue or building built to help us remember famous people; a memorial.

mountain (moun'tain) A high, rocky piece of land, often with steep sides. A mountain is higher than a hill.

museum (mu·se'um) A place that shows interesting and valuable things from art, science, or other subjects.

natural resource (nat'u·ral re'source') Something in or on the earth that people use. Land, trees, water, and oil are some natural resources.

neighborhood (neigh'bor·hood') A small community within a city or town.

north (north) The direction toward the North Pole.

northeast (north·east') The direction between north and east.

northwest (north·west') The direction between north and west.

ocean (o'cean) Any of the four largest water areas on the earth.

248

oil (oil) An important natural resource that comes from the ground. It is used for fuel and many other things.

pedestrian (pe·des'tri·an) A person who walks.

physical map (phys'i·cal map) A map that shows what the land looks like.

plain (plain) Low, flat land.

plateau (pla·teau') High, flat land.

population (pop'u·la'tion) The number of people living in a place.

President (Pres'i·dent) The elected leader of our country.

preview (pre'view) To see ahead of time.

produce (pro·duce') To make something.

product (prod'uct) Anything that is grown or raised on a farm or made in a factory.

railroad (rail'road') A system of tracks on which trains travel.

rainfall (rain'fall') The amount of rain that falls.

ranch (ranch) A large farm where cattle, sheep, or horses are raised.

recreation (rec're·a'tion) A way to have fun.

recreation community (rec're·a'tion com·mu'ni·ty) A community that provides a way or ways for people to have fun.

residential (res'i·den'tial) Having to do with homes.

restaurant (res'tau·rant) A place where people buy and eat meals.

restore (re·store') To make an old place look the way it did when it was first built.

road map (road map) A map that shows the roads in a certain area.

scientist (sci'en·tist) A person who studies the world in which we live.

sea farming (sea farm'ing) A way of raising fish in certain areas of the ocean as a source of food.

sell (sell) To give something in return for money.

service center (ser'vice cen'ter) A place where many goods and services are provided.

services (ser'vic·es) Jobs that people do for others.

settlement (set'tle·ment) A place where people begin a small community in a new land.

settler (set'tler) A person who moves to a new land.

shelter (shel'ter) A place to live.

shipping center (ship'ping cen'ter) A place where many important goods are brought in and out on ships.

skyscraper (sky'scrap'er) A tall building that has many floors.

south (south) The direction toward the South Pole.

southeast (south·east') The direction between south and east.

southwest (south·west') The direction between south and west.

space city (space cit'y) A city of the future that would be built in space.

sphere (sphere) A round object, shaped like a ball.

suburb (sub'urb') A community smaller than a city and located near a city.

surveyor (sur·vey'or) A person who measures the size, shape, and boundaries of an area of land.

swamp (swamp) Soft, spongy land, sometimes with trees, that is often covered with water.

symbol (sym′bol) A drawing that stands for a real thing.

temperature (tem′per·a·ture′) How warm or cold it is.

terrace (ter′race) A step built on the slope of a mountain to hold water or provide level land for crops.

textile (tex′tile′) Cloth.

thermometer (ther·mom′e·ter) An instrument for measuring temperature.

time line (time line) A graph that shows when things happened.

town (town) A community that has more people than a farm and fewer people than a city.

trade (trade) The buying and selling of goods.

transportation (trans′por·ta′tion) Any way to move people and goods from place to place. Airplanes, buses, and cars are forms of transportation.

valley (val′ley) The low land between hills or mountains.

village (vil′lage) A small community.

wanderer (wan′der·er) A person who moves from place to place.

weather (weath′er) What it is like outside. Weather includes temperature, wind, rain, snow, sunshine, and many other things.

west (west) A direction. West is to the left of a person facing north.

Index

The following Index will help you find the pages that give information about important people, places, and things. The subjects listed in the Index are in the order of the alphabet, just as they are in the Glossary.

Notice that in the Index people are listed with their last names first. For example, if you wanted to read about Benjamin Franklin, you would look under the last name, **Franklin.** Under what name would you look if you wanted to find out something about Pierre L'Enfant? Practice using the Index to find important information in this book.

Acknowledgments

Artwork

Colrus, John, 191, 192, 193
Dyess, John, 114, 115, 116, 117, 118, 180, 181
Gold, Ethel, 133, 135, 152, 183, 228, 243
Killgrew, John, 79, 87, 89, 90, 91, 103, 120,
121, 126, 129, 134, 136, 138, 162, 222
Newman, Deirdre, 36, 37, 66, 67, 94, 99, 125,
147, 245
O'Reilly, Michael, 34, 35, 93, 166, 168, 170,
171, 173, 175, 202, 205
Powers, Tom, 242

Photographs

Cover: Ellis Herwig/The Image Bank
Page 7: National Aeronautics and Space
Administration
15, 16: Michal Heron
20: Tom Stack/Tom Stack &
Associates
23: Ray Atkeson
24: left, Keith Gunnar/Bruce Coleman,
Inc.; right, Michal Heron
25: top, Michal Heron; bottom, Robert
Frerck
26: left, John Zoiner/Peter Arnold,
Inc.; right, Peter Menzel/Stock
Boston, Inc.
27: top, Robert Frerck; bottom,
Charles Henneghien/Bruce
Coleman, Inc.
29: top left, Hans Wendler/The Image
Bank; top right, Ray
Boultinghouse; bottom left, E. R.
Degginger; bottom right, Robert
Frerck
31: top left, Grant Heilman; top right,
Robert Frerck; bottom left, E. R.
Degginger; bottom right, John
Running/Stock Boston
32: left, Walter Frerck; right, Cary
Wolinsky/Stock Boston, Inc.
33: top, Vince Streano/Bruce
Coleman, Inc.; bottom, John Elk,
III/Bruce Coleman, Inc.
39: Robert Frerck
41: top left, top right, and bottom left,
Grant Heilman; bottom right, Bess
Bottoms
42: left, Robert Frerck; top right, Grant
Heilman; bottom right, Nicholas de
Vore, III/ Bruce Coleman, Inc.
43: top and bottom right, Grant
Heilman; bottom left, Jonathan T.
Wright/Bruce Coleman, Inc.
44: top, Ken Lax; bottom, E. R.
Degginger
45, 46: Grant Heilman
47: top, Carter Hamilton/Nancy Palmer
Agency, Inc.; bottom, National Film
Board of Canada
48: Ken Lax
49, 50: Robert Frerck
51: top, Brooks/Monkmeyer; bottom
left and right, Robert Frerck
52: Michal Heron
53: Charlton Photos
54: Courtesy Texas Rice Association
55: left, Courtesy of Texas Rice
Association; right, Ken Lax
57: top left, Robert Frerck; top right,
Grant Heilman; bottom, Charlton
Photos
59: W. E. Ruth/Bruce Coleman, Inc.

60: top left, Norman Myers/Bruce
Coleman, Inc.; top right, Florita
Botts/Nancy Palmer Agency, Inc.;
bottom left, Walter H. Hodge/Peter
Arnold, Inc.; bottom right, Harvey
Lloyd/Peter Arnold, Inc.
61: top, John Elk, III/Bruce Coleman,
Inc.; bottom, Florita Botts/Nancy
Palmer Agency, Inc.
62: V. Rastelli/Woodfin Camp
63: Delta Willis/Bruce Coleman, Inc.
64: left, Terry Madison/The Image
Bank; right, © Menschenfreund
68: left, National Film Board of
Canada; center and right, Grant
Heilman
69: top left, E. R. Degginger; top right,
Jonathan Wright/Bruce Coleman,
Inc.; bottom, Charles Henneghien/
Bruce Coleman, Inc.
71: E. R. Degginger/Bruce Coleman,
Inc.
73: top left and right and bottom right,
Michal Heron; bottom left, David
Overcash/Bruce Coleman, Inc.
74: Kenneth Murray/Nancy Palmer
Agency, Inc.
75: Bill Brooks/Bruce Coleman, Inc.
76, 77, 78, 80: Robert Frerck
82: left, E. R. Degginger; right, Robert
Frerck
83: Shostal Associates
85: Tom Stack & Associates
86: Victoria Beller-Smith
88: John Running/Stock Boston
90: Michal Heron
95: Courtesy of Cannon Mills Company
96: Courtesy of North Carolina Textile
Manufacturers Association
97: Arthur d'Arazien/The Image Bank
101: Robert Frerck
104: left, Clyde Smith/Peter Arnold,
Inc.; right, Cary Wolinsky/Stock
Boston, Inc.
106: National Aeronautics and Space
Administration
108: left, Victoria Beller-Smith; right,
© Menschenfreund
109: Courtesy of Boeing
110: top left, Michal Heron; top right, N.
Shah/Shostal Associates; bottom,
Gabe Palmer/The Image Bank
111: top, © Menschenfreund; middle,
George Hall/Woodfin Camp;
bottom, Don Brewster/Bruce
Coleman, Inc.
112: Victoria Beller-Smith
113: left, Minneapolis Star; right, M.
Timothy O'Keefe/Bruce Coleman,
Inc.
123: F. Roiter/The Image Bank
124: R. Thompson/Photo Trends
131: Rick McIntyre/Tom Stack &
Associates
139: California Historical Society/Title
Insurance & Trust Co.
140: top left, California Historical
Society/Title Insurance & Trust
Co.; top right, Courtesy of
Lockheed; bottom, The Bettmann
Archive Inc.
141: Robert Frerck
142: The Bettmann Archive Inc.
144: top, Joachim Messerschmidt/
Bruce Coleman, Inc.; bottom,
© Menschenfreund

145: Cary Wolinsky/Stock Boston, Inc.
150: John Elk, III/Bruce Coleman, Inc.
153: Shostal Associates
154: left, Jehangir Gazdar/Woodfin
Camp; right, Burt Glinn/Magnum
155: Jehangir Gazdar/Woodfin Camp
157: top left, Courtesy of Boeing; right,
Jehangir Gazdar/Woodfin Camp;
bottom left, Bison Archives
159: Helena Kolda
161: D. C. Lowe/Shostal Associates
163: Historical Pictures Service
165: Walter Frerck
167: National Aeronautics and Space
Administration
169, 172, 174: Walter Frerck
182: Robert Frerck
185: Library of Congress
187: Historical Pictures Service
188, 190, 194: Helena Kolda
195: left, Historic Savannah Foundation;
right, Louisville Landmarks
Commission
196: Helena Kolda
199: National Geographic Society
201: Dick Durrance/Woodfin Camp
203: left, The Bettmann Archive Inc.;
right, Historical Pictures Service
204: Library of Congress
206: National Archives
208: National Aeronautics and Space
Administration
209: top, Wm. Clark/National Park
Service; bottom, U.S. Treasury
Dept.
210: top left and bottom left, National
Park Service; right, National
Archives
211: left, Wm. Clark/National Park
Service; right, National Archives
215: Robert Frerck/Woodfin Camp
216, 217, 218: Reproduced with the
permission of the Commonwealth
Government of Australia
219: top, Robert Frerck/Woodfin Camp;
bottom, Robert Frerck/Woodfin
Camp
220: top, R. Gordon/Atoz/Van Cleve;
bottom, Ian Cooper/Canberra
225: Wayne Thom
226: left, The Bettmann Archive Inc.;
right, Courtesy of General Motors
227: top left and bottom left, The
Bettmann Archive Inc.; top right
and bottom right, Michal Heron
229: Robert Frerck
230, 232: Michal Heron
233: Courtesy of Constantin A. Rebeiz/
University of Illinois
234: Sekai Bunka Photo
237: Cumbernauld Development
Corporation
241: Buckminster Fuller

Maps

Page 239: Adapted with permission of Howard
Research and Development
Corporation

256

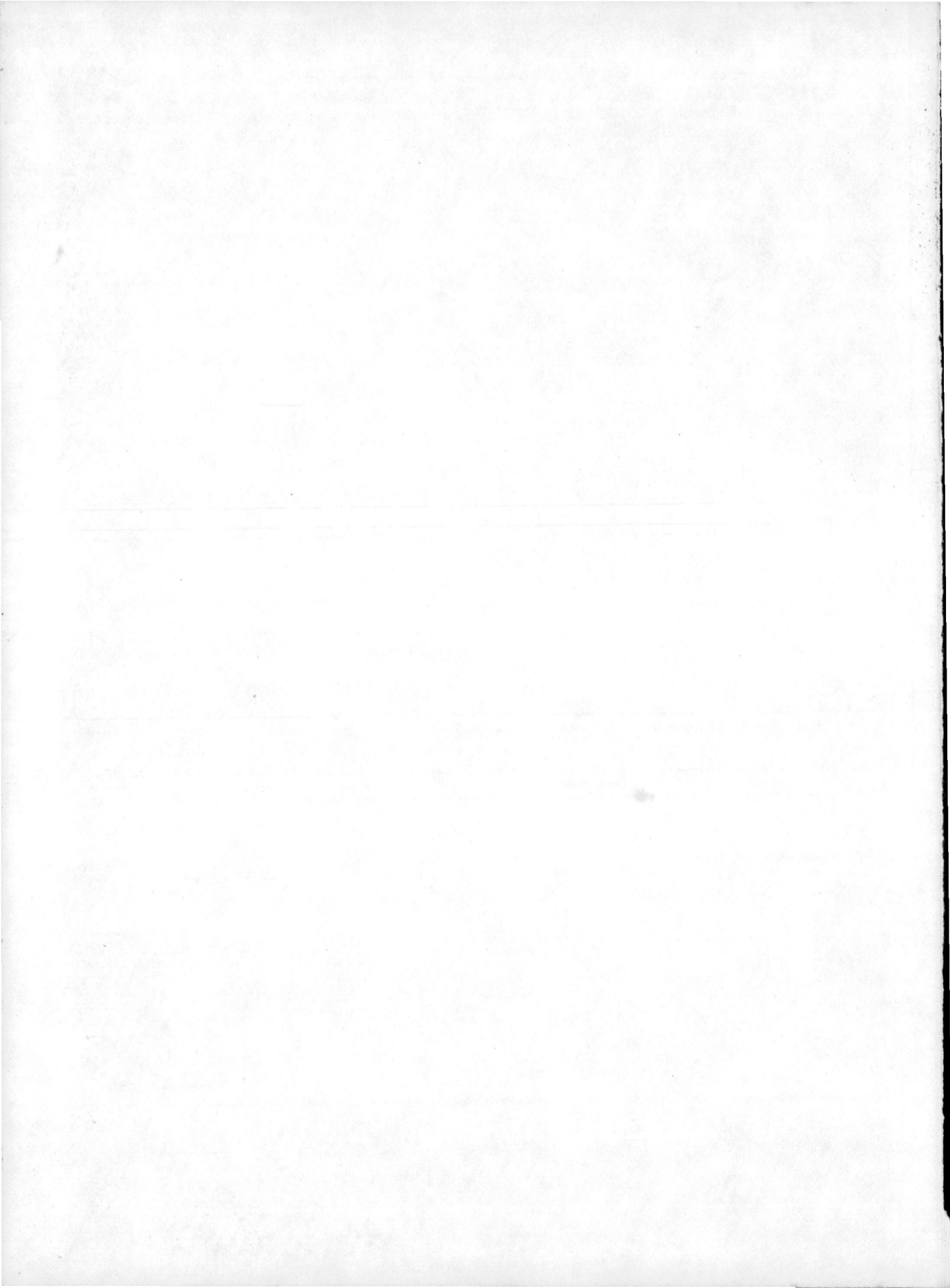